DISGRACEFULLY
Yours

DISGRACEFULLY *Yours*

More New Ideas for Getting the Most Out of Life

by
The Hen Co-op

Photographs by Marianne Gontarz

The Crossing Press, Freedom, CA 95019

First published in 1995 in the U.K. by
Judy Piatkus (Publishers) Ltd.

Published in 1996 in the U.S. by the Crossing Press, by permission.

Book design by Sheryl Karas
Cover design by Victoria May
Photographs (except for portraits of the authors) by Marianne Gontarz
Contemporary photographs of authors by Douglas Cape, except those of Anne and Shirley,
     which are by Vaughan Melzer
Illustrations by Angela Martin
Printed in the U.S.A.

Women in the cover photos are Shirley, Chaya and Minnie

ISBN 0-89594-804-4

Contents

Anne Woolf hopes to reach her three-score-and-ten years on International Women's Day in the year 2000 and intends to celebrate with her Hen friends, with seven days of feasting and dancing. Until then, she wants to fly her kite, play pooh-sticks and collect horse chestnuts into an active and disgraceful second childhood.

At 63, **Barbara Tayler** is still waiting to become a grown-up. Like a chameleon, she changes mood and colour according to background and companions. But on good days she feels that ageing is a cheerful process and that life still holds many joys, not the least of which is the publication of a second book. "What next?" she wonders.

Edith Redstone was born seventy-six years ago in New York. She arrived in London with her British husband in 1944 and has been here ever since. In the next half century, they had two children and eventually six grandchildren. With the recent death of her husband, she is in the process of trying to compose a new life for herself.

Mary Cooper, born in 1924, says she is surprised to be enjoying her life so much at the age of 70 and is sorry it won't go on for ever. She was always a late developer—a degree at 41, a career in Adult Education, divorced after four daughters, and 34 years of marriage. And she still wants to write the book that will change the world.

Maxine Myers has just celebrated her 65th birthday by retiring from her job. She lives in Santa Cruz, California, in a one-room converted garage, where she has been known to house several Hens at a time. Future plans include enjoying her seven grandchildren, doing as much travelling as her pension will allow, indulging her addiction to *The Guardian* crossword and being as disgraceful as possible.

The billboard sign asked "Is there life after death?" Almost 65, **Shirley Meredeen** prefers to ponder the question "Is there life **before** death?" and to prove the answer to be YES. As a writer, mother, grandmother, mature student, counselor and trainer, every cranny of her life is filled. She is determined not to depart this life with the words "if only" on her breath.

Introduction

Dear Reader

When we wrote our first book, *Growing Old Disgracefully*, we had no idea that it would touch a nerve in so many people. We did not and still do not think of ourselves as experts, we simply wrote about our own experiences and our journeys to the lives we now lead. We told about how we had met three years earlier at a workshop called *Growing Old Disgracefully* and how we wrote the book to share the ideas and the fun we found there. We described the process of six old women doing something we had never done before.

We put forth our definitions of what it means to us to grow old disgracefully. We offered ideas and suggestions for finding the courage to say "It's my turn now" and to take steps towards making the rest of life more fulfilling. We did not want to give advice, because we don't always know what's right for ourselves, much less for anyone else. We just spoke from our hearts as honestly as we could in the hopes that other women might find some insights of their own through our words.

And they did. So many people recognized their own experiences, thoughts and feelings in what we had written that we were overwhelmed with responses. Within a few months we had received over a thousand letters from women wanting to know what to do about their lives, how to link up with others who wanted the same, how to grow old disgracefully in their present circumstances.

It became clear that, even if we had thought we were able to give advice, we could not answer each person individually. We wrote to let people know that there were others who felt the same way, and we gave them names of women in their geographic areas for contacts. There are now dozens of ongoing Growing Old Disgracefully Network groups in existence, mostly in Britain, but also in the US, Canada, Australia, and New Zealand. (In Chapter 8 you will find ideas about how to join or start a group and some activities you might want to pursue.)

As we read the correspondence, it became clear that many women were expressing similar concerns and questions, so we decided to write this second book as a way to explore some of the issues that seemed to crop up most often. We have structured our writings around the letters and their themes, but rather than using any one person's question, we start each chapter with a composite letter which represents the most common concerns we heard. All names are fictitious and the words are our own, but the ideas expressed are representative of what women say in their letters to us. In cases where we felt that topics were out of the realm of our own personal experiences, we invited other women to contribute to the book. We would like to thank Jenny Betts, June Green, Sally O'Connor, Marie Mayall and Irene Smithe for sharing their experiences.

We begin by introducing ourselves to you. Instead of repeating our chronological, short autobiographies as they appeared in *Growing Old Disgracefully*, we chose instead to tell you something that would give you a look into how we see ourselves now as we reflect on our lives.

As we progress through the chapters, you will find us addressing themes of the gap between expectations and reality, the narrowing and expanding of choices in later life, the balancing act of trying to assert our own needs and wishes after a lifetime of catering to everyone else's, making changes in relationships, especially when your partner is a "grumpy old bore," and the loneliness that seems so poignant in old age. And of course the big question of how to deal with changing bodies and sexuality was one we could not ignore.

We think that what we mean by growing old disgracefully will emerge from our writings. You will see that it is not about denying age but about celebrating it; it is not about mutilating our bodies in the name of beauty, but about seeing our bodies as beautiful the way they are; it is not about being selfish, but is about rediscovering and nurturing the self; it is not about trying to live up to anyone else's expectations, but about smashing through the stereotypes of what it means to be an old woman.

Topics such as death, mourning, ill health, and becoming dependent on others do not seem to be part of growing old disgracefully, but in Chapter 6 we try to show that even these painful subjects can be discussed when you have others you trust enough to share your vulnerabilities. We have had some good laughs and a few tears over our own increasingly fragile conditions, but by letting each other know how we perceive the changes in ourselves, we discovered that we are not alone in our feelings.

Growing old disgracefully by definition must include sharing our experiences with others so that each of us knows she is not alone in dealing with the issues of old age. The feminist poet, essayist and novelist Audre Lorde called the ways we have been kept from speaking out to each other "the tyrannies of silence." She speaks of her discovery:

> I was going to die, if not sooner then later, whether or not I had ever spoken myself. My silences had not protected me. Your silence will not protect you. But for every real word spoken...I had made contact with other women...And it was the concern and caring of all those women which gave me strength and enabled me to scrutinize the essentials of my living.*

Being close to both old and new friends has been our lifeline, giving us the support needed, as Lorde says, to find and use the real words which "scrutinize the essentials" of our lives. We have discovered that even at those times when it seems all that lies ahead is a downhill slope, supportive friends can help you maintain a positive attitude and find the choices that will keep you feeling good about yourself, an essential ingredient in growing old disgracefully.

We hope that by sharing our experiences with you in our "real words" throughout this book, we will encourage you to grow and flourish as you continue towards a disgraceful old age. We wish you much joy and courage along the way.

Disgracefully yours,

The Hen Co-op

Once again we have not allowed a distance of 6,000 miles to separate Maxine in California from the rest of us in England. We would like to express our thanks for her special contribution in writing the introductions to the chapters.

*"The Transformation of Silence into Language and Action," essay in *Sister Outsider* (1984, The Crossing Press, California).

Self-Portraits

You may wonder who we are, since The Hen Co-op appears to be the author of this book. We write under a group name because the library cataloguing system restricted us to two authors and none of us would agree to have her name listed unless the other five were included too. Since we had met in 1989 at a women's holiday and study center called The Hen House where the idea for our first book was conceived, we chose to call ourselves The Hen Co-op, without realizing how much of who we are would become tied up in its many layers of meanings.

The Hen Co-op is our collective identity now, and it would be hard for any of us to imagine not being a part of it. You may notice as you read our self-portraits that each of us has found great joy and comfort in this group identity, although maintaining the connection has not always been easy. Geographic distances, differences of opinions, and personal feelings have all interrupted the process, but the bonds have been strengthened by working through problems together.

So who are we as individuals? What can we tell you about us? In our previous book, *Growing Old Disgracefully*, we introduced ourselves by means of short autobiographies in a chapter which we called "Telling Our Stories." Because we believe that each woman has a story of courage and strength to tell, we did not set ourselves up as role models or think that we were special. We had each lived a woman's life, which included the peaks and valleys, the fulfilments and the disappointments of what we saw as ordinary existence. Telling our stories set us on a path of self-discovery that is still in progress. We continue to share memories with each other as a way to understand who we are and how we can move ahead.

When we were deciding how we wanted to introduce ourselves here, we thought we would share with you how we identify ourselves at this point in time. We may or may not be accurate in our self-assessments, but writing our stories in this way has given us a chance to step back and look at ourselves, warts and all. It is a process we highly recommend. So here we are, six disgraceful old women ranging in age from 63 to 76, still looking for new ways to smash the stereotypes of what old women are supposed to be.

The Unexpurgated Version
Anne

The last time I wrote a short autobiography, this gleaming, successful woman emerged. Since then, I've received a shock, a nasty setback. The picture I have been carrying around of myself for years as a calm, clever, relaxed, sweet-natured person, always caring for others, is false. I am beginning to know my demons and have discovered an imperfect creature who is competitive, envious, spiteful and disapproving. Like bad breath, it's something even your best friends never tell you!

Can I live with this new imperfect me? This me who wants to excel, to be the best mother, sister, friend, writer, painter, dancer? This me who envies and resents those who are better, kinder, more talented, more loving? This me who lets people down? Yes, I think I can because I am trying to accept these imperfections in myself as I try to accept them in others. I know I can enjoy all these relationships and experiences for themselves, and I don't have to be better. Which reminds me of a verse written by a school-friend in my autograph book when I was twelve which shows what goals we set ourselves even then:

> *Good, better, best,*
> *But never rest*
> *Till your good is better*
> *And your better best!*

So any previous lines I have written about myself describing a woman only virtuous and kind should be deleted and way made for a truer, more rounded person. This is the unexpurgated version.

As the oldest of three children, I always wanted to be my parents' favorite. In school, I always wanted to be teacher's pet, and even worked hard at mathematics in my quest for favor. As a Patrol Leader in the Girl

Guides I wanted my patrol to outrun the others, to collect more badges, to do more good deeds.

At work I wanted to be the best social worker with special insights and deep intuition which no one else could even glimpse. As the wife of my most handsome husband, I wanted to have the perfect home, everything in its place, my dinner parties known for their exotic and delicious dishes. As a mother I wanted to be seen to live for my two beautiful children, to respond to their every wish and whim. Now retired, I want to be seen as strong and self-sufficient, able to cope on my own with all life's demands. Only perfection will do!

I don't want to paint only the dark side of my nature because that would not be the whole truth either, but it feels more honest, in fact quite a relief, to acknowledge that both sides exist, and to share them as my introduction to my "self." After all, why pretend?

Having got that off my chest, I will tell you briefly who I am. A woman alone in the autumn of her life, who enjoys her solitude, but is sometimes lonely. A woman who loves the natural world of plants, trees, birds and rainbows. A woman who loves to walk, swim and dance, but also to read, listen to music or just "be." A woman who is searching for the quiet, still part of herself.

I find it difficult to take risks and break away from old behavior patterns, but I do want to put convention aside, to be spontaneous and to grow old disgracefully. It's a struggle.

Anne

My Story
Barbara

Once upon a time there was a little girl called Barbara Shirley Samson, who had a Mom but no Dad and spent her childhood in other people's houses. She was a somewhat shy, clever, sulky, solitary child, who became a hardworking, high-achieving, romantic adolescent. At twenty she married and became Mrs Barbara Tayler, wife then mother, energetic and well-organized, politically active and involved, holding down a job and bringing up four children. After the breakdown of her marriage her next role was that of a single parent, juggling hard to keep all those balls in the air while maintaining some semblance of a life of her own. As each of the children flew from the nest in turn, Barbara's work became more and more central to her life. She has often marvelled at the serendipity of finding a job which fitted around having children and held her interest for over thirty years, a job which was both stimulating and worthwhile. But the years rolled by and at the age of sixty Barbara retired and entered a new phase of her life—a woman growing old and living alone. Somewhere inside her all those earlier incarnations still exist, they reassert their right to exist in times of stress or emotion. Sometimes she feels closer to the little girl or the romantic adolescent than to the mother at the hub of the family—more in touch with her own needs and able to give herself permission to enjoy everything she can in life.

There you have my very brief history. What am I like now?

Well, I can't bear to be left out of anything. Whatever it is I want to be part of it. I have a great need to be an insider, one of the chosen, in the know. So I have a compulsion to volunteer for jobs but then often resent being overloaded and tend to let everybody know it. I may appear to be well-organized but it's a con-trick, open any drawer and you will find numerous packets of photographs, undated, unsorted into albums, many with initials on their backs indicating who wanted copies which were never made because I mislaid the negatives. You will find letters unanswered, outdated programs for concerts I meant to book for or meetings I firmly intended to attend. I recently found a drawer full of forgotten clothes I had packed away when I did a house-swap. Well, that gave me a pleasant surprise!

You would think that, after all these years, I would be resigned to these failings. But no. I constantly resolve to sort the photographs, book tickets as soon as programs arrive and answer letters within a reasonable time. Maybe I will—next year.

I try not to be a grouch but I do sink into self-pity at times. I did not choose to live alone in my old age but I am not sure that I could live with somebody else after so long alone, although times with the Hen Co-op are great and we have all managed to remain friends after sharing kitchens, bathrooms and living space, however confined. I love the feeling of togetherness generated on these occasions but I am always happy to be back home in my own little house.

The presence of grandchildren in my life has brought great joy. As the saying goes—if I'd known how much fun grandchildren are I would have had them first! I love their endearing personalities and enquiring minds; the feel of their arms around my neck and soft cheeks against mine fill me with emotion. I do realize that I am a lucky woman. My daughter and two of my sons live near enough for me to have close contact with them and with all four of my grandchildren. But, remembering how much I resented unasked-for advice and criticism from my mother, aunt and mother-in-law, I try to keep a balance between loving concern and separation. "What a paragon!" you may say, and you would be right to say it skeptically. Because, of course, I don't always get it right. Sometimes, in an unguarded moment, a remark slips out and I groan inwardly as I realize that it is just the kind of thing I vowed never to say. But I do try.

I enjoy chatting over news, views and reactions with friends. Less charitably, it could be called gossip but that is a term I dislike because it is so often used to put women down. I like to think that I share a womanly interest in the lives and feelings of others—but sometimes I have to admit to a wicked enjoyment in sharing a particularly juicy morsel. Perhaps I am not really a nice person at heart? Well, I'll have to leave it to my friends to judge that.

So, here I am, at sixty-three, and most of the time life feels good, full of fun and challenges still to be met. I can vividly remember thinking that people of forty were over the hill but now I realize that it's all a trick of perspective, the hill always lies ahead of you—that is, until you finally reach it.

Writing has become the central focus which I had feared would be missing from my life after I retired from the job I had loved so much. Life has turned out to be fun, much more fun than I could ever have expected. But the older I get, the clearer it becomes that my core of self-doubt never really goes away. However, when I get positive affirmation and love, much of the time I have a niggling feeling that I could be found out, that some horrible secret lies hidden. Whatever that secret might be, I hope I take it with me to my grave.

Barbara

Tree of life
Edith

Here I am at the age of 76 at the top of the tree. When I look down, I see my son and daughter with each of their families spread out on the lower branches. Not so long ago before he died my husband would have shared that upper space with me. With his death, I have come almost full circle as I am once more on my own. How did I arrive at that high place so quickly, having travelled such a long way from my original beginnings in New York, to England, marriage, children and their children, my grandchildren?

Until my marriage, the journey often appeared slow and unfulfilling. Trapped by my family's struggle for survival during the Depression in the late 1920s and 30s, I sometimes felt completely stymied, unable to get on with my life. When I look at my diaries for that period, I seem to have done little more than attend school, read, go to the movies and grumble. There was no joy, every page carries a complaint, an unhappiness at home. I try to remember whether it was a period of unremitting dullness and gloom or just an adolescent sounding off.

Happily, time doesn't stand still and movement, however slow it may have seemed then, was gradually getting me to another place. How strange that World War II proved to be the catalyst which altered the tempo of my life, quickening the pace. I still can't believe that half a century has gone by since I first arrived in England. Yet so much has happened in that time. A born and bred New Yorker arriving in wartime London, learning to live with unaccustomed deprivations as well as a different social scene wasn't easy, but I slipped into the postwar period with far less difficulty. I must have been so absorbed in my family and the process of adjusting to a new way of life that I didn't notice the years gliding by.

Of course there were ups and downs; no marriage of over fifty years survives without them. We were an average nuclear family of two children, a boy and a girl, eventually leading to grandchildren. Not without some traumas, we all came through without any real damage. Perhaps because in the main it had been such a long and loving period, it all seemed to go quickly. I keep wishing for a time clock, so I could turn it back for a longer look. With my husband's retirement, however, the pattern began to change. He was then just over 75, older than the usual retiring age. This change greatly affected me. Until then I had been able to go my own way, follow my own interests. No structured career but a variety of stimulating occupations kept me involved outside the home. Over the years with this freedom I had established an identity, separate from home and family.

My husband's identity disappeared along with his work. With very few outside friendships and unable to create a new structure, he began to invade my space. My established pattern began to crumble. I was no longer a liberated woman and I became resentful of his increasing need for my presence. It was at that point I went to the Hen House, partly for respite, but also for the opportunity to discuss my problem with like-minded women.

Some of the rest is history. It was there I met the five women who were to radically alter my life as well as to help restore the balance to it, at least for a time. When my husband became ill a few years later, I knew I wanted to spend this time with him. Another reordering of my life was needed, especially as his condition worsened. My main activity was with the writing group, where the writing continued and where there were always sympathetic hands to hold me when the tears began to flow. My own immediate family was always there for me and my husband as well in so many different ways. Both groups came together for an unforgettable time, just after the New Year in Devon. My husband went to stay with our son and his family on their farm, while I was with three of our writing group in a cottage nearby. As our daughter and her two girls also live only a short distance away, they visited him daily, as I did too, every afternoon and from time to time, my sister writers as well. The groups merged around him; he was the focus of it all. There he would sit, either in his wheelchair or something more comfortable; listening to the songs of Piaf or the Beatles, keeping up with the radio Archers, or watching the ice-skating championships on

TV; never alone, always with the people he cared about and who cared about him. It was a memorable time for all of us who were part of it. It must have been the high point for him because soon after we returned to London, he began to go downhill. He died very peacefully at home in the middle of March.

Now I am in the process of composing a new life for myself alone at the top of that tree but with supporting branches below me.

Edith

Queen Bee
Mary

Now this is Mary—she's just been celebrating her 70th birthday—she has to keep reminding herself "I'm old and that's how people see me!" No matter how she tries to dress herself up—and how hard she tries—that's still the truth. She's 70!

And she's still smoking—to the disgust of the rest of the members of the Hen Co-op. So every now and again she makes excuses and creeps off on her own to have a cigarette.

It's hard being a smoker, she says—especially sharing the same space as these other virtuous Hens. It's the same when she visits any of her four daughters. She has to stand at the back door come rain, snow or shine.

She has some other secretive habits as well—like wrapping her head in a scarf when she goes to bed—very quaint and not endearing—she'd rather not be seen early in the morning.

But life's often difficult for Mary. She's 70 as I said but she still hates missing things!

She used to work in Adult Education and was the Queen Bee at a shabby little Adult Education Centre in one of the most deprived areas of the Northeast of England, until she retired in 1988. That's when she started leading the Growing Old Disgracefully Courses for women at the Hen House—the original Women's Study and Holiday Center in Lincolnshire. And she still wants to be the Queen Bee—because she can't bear missing out!

But when it comes to doing any of the work associated with the Growing Old Disgracefully Network—like looking after the finances or keeping track of the members' addresses—well, it's difficult living so far away, she says, and scuttles off back North.

It's cheaper living up there of course. It leaves Mary more money to spend on her outfits, or getting her hair done into a frizzy perm, and more time to write the novel she'll tell you about if you give her the chance. Ask her what it's about and she'll say it's about six old women telling each other disgraceful stories. It's not got sex in it but it is about sex, because Mary thinks she knows a lot about sex. She may have had various sexual partners in her lifetime but that doesn't mean to say she understands much about MEN—because she doesn't and to tell you the truth, she never has! She married the first likely man who was anything like serious about her—partly because she thought she was pregnant when they got engaged and then didn't break it off when she found she wasn't because she didn't want to get left on the shelf.

Did she choose to have children then? Not really. But she didn't want to miss out on that either—so she made a hole in the cap with a safety pin and waited to see what would happen!

Well, four daughters happened and Mary says they were the best things that ever could have happened. And the years passed, not all happy ones. In those days you didn't tell anyone, not your best friend, certainly not your mother, that your marriage had been a dreadful mistake. They must have known but they didn't say anything either.

What was the point? Where else was there to go?

But in the 60s and 70s things began to change. Women started talking to each other. The personal became political. But Mary didn't leave her husband until she'd been married for 34 years and her youngest daughter was nearly 20—not because there was anyone else, but because she couldn't bear it any longer. She'd managed to get a university degree when she was 41 and from then on she could be financially independent. That's what made the difference—her own money—not a lot but enough to buy a small terraced house near where she worked. She's lived on her own since then and says she wouldn't have it any other way.

So now there's no sexual passion in her life. But there can be more to passion than sex, Mary says. Being 70 doesn't stop her holding strong opinions of course, or expressing them passionately on any subject that comes up, with some vigor if not quite as well as a Queen Bee should. She still fancies herself as a Marxist and a feminist—though now in 1994 not so many people want to use those words or to hear them either.

So now and again Mary says—I've had enough politics and such— I don't want to spend the last few years I have left fighting battles that are not going to be won in my lifetime, if ever.

At this stage in my life—she says—I want to do the things that I enjoy doing most and being with the people whose company I enjoy the most. I want to see more of my sister, my twin sister—because we've had to spend so much of our lives living far apart. And I want to go on travelling to different countries while I still have some time, some money and some health left to enjoy it.

And isn't she right?

So what about setting out to write another *Growing Old Disgrace-fully* book? Is this the most enjoyable way of spending precious time Mary asks herself. It'll take hours! It's not just getting the writing done, it's all the time it takes to put off the writing—another cuppa, a walk because we all need more exercise, another meeting that cannot be missed—is Mary going to make it?

If she can't bear to miss out she'll have to make the effort, have to forget about the novel, have to spend the money, and have to get herself to London and be ready to join in.

I can't have the others writing the book without me—Mary says.

So—here she is. Now—on with the writing and long live the Hen Co-op!

Mary

Am I Who I Have Always Been?
Maxine

As I write this, I have just passed my 65th birthday, a significant life-marker, it seems. In the US it is the age to retire, to collect Social Security, and to qualify for Medicare health benefits and all senior discounts. It is the no-doubts-about-it, you-are-now-officially-OLD year. So should I feel differently about myself now? Will I be a different person? Who am I now and how will I know if I've changed? I guess a good place to start would be to try to compare the way I see myself now to my recollections of myself in the past. Are there any threads that run through my life, showing that there is continuity in my identity?

A vivid memory from my early childhood in Texas: barely able to read or write, and not having money for proper writing paper, I take long strips of toilet tissue and scribble make-believe speeches on them. I stand on the the steps of the front porch delivering this imaginary speech to an imaginary audience.

Later: taking parts in plays at the School of Expression, my primary extra-curricular activity. Winning a state-wide competition for "declamation." (I still have the trophy which now serves as a pencil holder next to my telephone.)

In my teens, joining a new theatrical troupe, performing in twenty or more plays, usually in comic relief roles.

Giving up theatre entirely when I moved from Texas to California at the age of 21. At least I thought I had given it up. I did not even set foot in a theatre for years, probably because unconsciously I knew that the proverbial "smell of the greasepaint" would attract me. I chose instead to play the role of wife and mother.

Years later I would help launch a new community theatre group, becoming a producer rather than acting. I threw myself into the project, giving far more time to it than I should have, given my other responsibilities, but I was convinced that I was doing the community a great service. That was the justification I gave myself, I guess, to convince myself that I was not just selfishly falling back into my passion for the dramatic. No, I had purged all that from my system, right?

I have never been quite sure about the connection, but the theatre group thrived while my marriage failed. Did I spend long hours at the theatre because I found my marriage intolerable, or did my spending long hours at the theatre weaken the marriage? Probably both, although I suspect it was more of the former.

After the divorce, I spent a few years trying to decide who I was and who I wanted to be, now that my identity as "wife" had been stripped away and the three children were growing up. I became a 40-year-old "hippie" of sorts, testing the waters of freedom. I did not consider that this was a form of play-acting at the time, but as I look back now at the costuming, the trying-on of new identities, the loosening of inhibitions (by natural and artificial means), I can see the dramatic possibilities.

When I reached a point where financially and emotionally I could no longer afford to drift along, I became a student. At first I had no specific goal in mind, but eventually I settled on a course of study in Communications. In the end I switched my Major to Sociology, which seemed a safer distance from anything having to do with acting or theatre, or so I thought, until it came time to write a dissertation, and I focused my research on the images of women in Hollywood films.

Now, many years later, having retired from the teaching profession, I finally admit that what I loved most about my job was being able to stand up in front of a classroom and have a captive audience. It was always a thrill, and even after I had taught for many years, I still got opening-night butterflies at the start of each new term.

I have moved on to a new identity as "author." It is recent enough that I still feel as if I am playing a role, and that as soon as the run is over, I will return to everyday life. But what has become clear to me and to my coauthors is that I am at my best and experience my highest levels of energy when we do public appearances and readings. No matter how tired I am, or how sick I feel, or how little zip I think I have, when it is time to be "on," I can sparkle with the best of them.

My coauthors can also attest to the fact that I frequently upstage them, hogging the spotlight as often and as long as possible. Luckily, they are good enough friends to tell me that it is time to give someone else the floor, although I suspect they are too nice to stop me as often as I need it.

Now that you know all this about me, you can understand why growing old disgracefully has so much appeal to me. I can show off as much as I like, or be as silly as I please. I can choose to go for starring roles in life, or try the occasional walk-on. And when it comes time for me to retire from the stage of life, I hope I can do it with a dramatic flair.

Applause, please, and curtain.

Becoming My Own Person
Shirley

I was born a boy. Don't get me wrong. It was all a big mistake. My father was at home looking after my sick brother the day that I was born. And the message he received from hospital was that he was the father of a second son. Whether he was disappointed when he discovered the truth, I never knew. But maybe it accounts for my later "tomboyish" antics. What a reflection on the period that I was called a tomboy—that there were clearly distinct roles for boys and girls and an active girl like me was considered as a *quasi* male.

My spontaneity, my sporting and physical activities, my energy and loud guffaws were not what was expected of a nice middle-class girl. I was always full of contradictions as I suppose I still am. While I ached to rebel I also wanted to conform. I wanted to be good at schoolwork, but I read comics hidden in my homework. I wanted my parents to be happy but I seemed to spend a good deal of my time prying them apart, fending off their glancing blows to each other. I wanted to be slim and beautiful but I ate greedily. I wanted to play the piano but hated practicing. I wanted to have lots of friends but often felt an outsider. I was full of enthusiasms but got bored as soon as I started something new and rarely carried an idea through.

My adolescence was continually postponed. As a would-be renegade in wartime London, I seemed to spend a good deal of time in shelters, whether they were in basements for taking exams, in brickbuilt ones when the sirens interrupted my journey home by bicycle, or at home when I slept in Anderson shelters.

Then came immediate employment at 18, early marriage, young motherhood, frequent home moves with an ambitious husband whom I supported twice through university, continued part-time work which expanded to full-time work as my marriage disintegrated, then separation and the main responsibility for two adolescent sons. There had been little time for frivolity.

I still battle with contradictions in myself but a long, healthy life has enabled me to learn from mistakes, consolidate and build on my varied experiences. Being a woman of many "shreds and patches," having had a foot in many doors, with an ability to think laterally, has often helped me to act as a useful and helpful resource for others.

So many of my characteristics have stayed the same but I'm amazed at one of the photos in my album. It shows me dressed for reporting on the press bench in my local newspaper days—wearing a hat! What an anachronism. How could I? I must have been still trying to attract the approval of my mother. No wonder I was teased and called "Mama Shirl" by all the other reporters so much younger than I. It has taken me a long time to become my own person. In those days I was a big fish in a tiny pond. My articles were signed and sometimes my photo accompanied them. That period of my life suited me perfectly. While I had stability as wife and mother, every day was filled with bits and pieces of other people's lives, fragments of which did not make a solid whole. Superficiality was all. It was the lack of depth and purpose to my career that made me switch at what I like to think was the half-way point of my life.

From then on I tried to fill in the gaps in my education which I missed earlier while racing intuitively from one thing to another. I now realize that that my urgency must have stemmed from an attempt to compensate for my unhappy childhood and an increasingly disturbed marriage. It is only since the marriage ended that I've built up my self-esteem and relaxed somewhat, though my earlier insecurities continually rear their ugly heads at times of stress.

Now I'm a woman alone and have been for 18 years. I have only myself to blame when things go wrong. In the main, life is good. I continue to work part time as a counselor, conciliator and administrator, both because I need the money and because I know I'm good at these things. I have a finger in various voluntary pies, which is consistent with my earlier life pattern but I'm more selective in my choices. Every day is full to overflowing with activities but I sometimes wonder what I get out of driving myself so hard.

When my solitary life began, my awakening did so too. Despite continued studies as a mature student and the anxieties about living and managing alone in reduced circumstances, life has got better all the time. My adolescence is at last beginning.

On a bad day I used to see myself as a procrastinator, a sluttish, untidy housewife who was content to watch the dust build up (believing in the theory that you don't notice after the first five years), halfway to losing my memory, domineering, an isolate. But nowadays when I wake I pull the bedclothes off in a positive mood and the picture is quite different. The procrastinator in me knows that I can get things done when working up against a deadline. What was the sluttish housewife is able to enjoy being lazy when I fancy, able to laugh it off should the unexpected visitor turn up. The memory loss is aggravating but maybe it is sometimes selective, protecting me from images I do not want to have with me all the time. And I'm not domineering really, just assertive when I believe in something deeply and want to get my point across. As to being an isolate, it's the self-contained me that's showing, capable of living alone, able to shut the door on others when I want to be alone, yet hospitably opening up at other times.

I'm 64, feeling quite unlike what I thought I would be at such an age, happier than before I was in my midlife crisis and went on to a safer place. As another disgraceful old woman has said: "I can take risks now I know I'm not going to die young!" Yet I'm greedy for life, to see my children and grandchildren blossom, for the new opportunities that each day brings—so my risks are not of the death-defying sort. They are concerned with living a full life, defying the humiliation heaped on old women, reversing the attitudes of centuries. I'm not asking a lot really! But someone's got to start, haven't they?

When I apply for a new passport next year, I will resist listing my occupation as "pensioner." No, the answer will definitely be "writer." Defying the odds, defying the assumptions about an old woman, into a new career at 64. How about that?

Shirley

CHAPTER ONE

I Never Expected It To Be Like This

Dear Hens,

I am 64 and was divorced a few years ago. I was very much in love with my husband and always believed that he loved me too. I would have said that we had a very happy marriage. When he left me for another woman half my age I was devastated. I had looked forward to sharing a happy and serene old age. Now I am facing my old age alone and with much less money than I would have had if we had stayed together. I never expected it to be like this.

Yours sincerely,

Brenda

Dear Brenda,

Throughout our lives we set up hopes and expectations for ourselves. Sometimes they come to pass, many times the reality of our lives diverges from what we had hoped it would be. When we reach certain milestones, or when something unexpected occurs, it is important to stop and reassess, to adjust our expectations based on the reality of the moment.

You must have had a severe blow to your dreams when your husband left. You expected a lifelong relationship, expected to be part of a couple "till death us do part." To be rejected is painful, to be rejected for a much younger woman reinforces the messages we get about age diminishing our worth as women.

Society is set up for coupledom, with messages all around us that in order to be whole, we must be in a one-to-one relationship. Of course, it can be wonderful when you have a loving, committed partner, someone who wants to make the relationship good for both. But that is not the only option for a fulfilled life. Many older women have been discovering that life alone can be liberating. You can make your own schedule, choose your own friends and activities, go and come as you please.

Adjusting to life on your own is made much easier when you have supportive people around you who will contradict your feelings of rejection and help you to see that not only are you OK, but that you still have a lot of life to live. Just because one man stopped loving you does not mean you are unlovable. Reach out to make new acquaintances and nurture those connections into friendships that will be affirming for you.

You do not have to give up hope or stop thinking about what kind of life you want to live, even though it must feel as if all your dreams have been erased. Common myth has it that old people have no future to anticipate, only an already lived past. But growing old disgracefully belies that myth and urges us to live looking forward, not backward. It is a realistic approach, acknowledging whatever your reality is in the present and allowing you a chance to set new hopes and priorities based on your current circumstances.

All of us in the Hen Co-op have experienced a change from what we expected our lives to be like. For example, Barbara and Anne describe their wedding days and how the future turned out to be much different from what they had envisioned, and Mary speaks of her feelings about revisiting the church where she was married. Anne thought she was on the way to an unexpected and exciting career, but her experience turned out to be quite different from her fantasy. Our pieces that follow reflect how we have come to think about these discrepancies between our expectations and reality in our relationships, careers, children and old age.

We certainly want to acknowledge your pain; we also want to offer you some suggestions for moving towards a sense of wholeness and a new identity as a person in your own right. One first small step is to acknowledge to yourself that you are not a "poor old thing." This is not easy when you have had such a major rejection, but it is essential. How you think about yourself will influence the way you live out your remaining years. What are your hopes now, given that "happily ever after" takes on a different meaning? When you approach the future with a sense of reality, you may find that there are lots of ways to make your life what you want it to be. You will find suggestions throughout this book, and we are sure that you will find many other resources for inspiration.

You mention your reduced financial circumstances. This can certainly be limiting, but there are many ways to enjoy life at little or no cost. You might not be able to acquire a lot of material possessions, but you can acquire new friends who like to do the same things you enjoy or develop new interests that cost little or nothing. It may sound simplistic and trite, but the old advice to develop a positive attitude is still our best key to success in finding new ways to make the best of our circumstances. Instead of "I can't do it" try substituting "This is a good idea, how can I make it happen?" Then enlist the help of others to see that it does happen.

Your bed was made for you, but you do not have to lie in it. Take risks, break old patterns. Reassess the "good old days" realistically. Were they really all that good? Are there things you want to change now? Give yourself time and space to grieve your loss. Have a healthy cry over the good memories as well as the bad. Your past experiences are what have made you the unique person you are today, and they will provide the foundation for moving on to growing old disgracefully. We hope our suggestions will start you on a new, joyful path.

Disgracefully yours,

The Hen Co-op

Love's Young Dream
Mary

Dear Brenda,

I really want to sympathize with how you must have been feeling writing this letter, because my own marriage didn't live up to my expectations either. The love that I thought was going to last for the rest of my life faded away at an early stage, when I was a lot younger than you are now. It was the loneliest time of my life. It took me many long and confusing years to come to terms with what happened then.

And I think many other women reading your letter will recognize the same sense of disappointment and feel cheated and let down as you do.

Your letter got me thinking and remembering…

How last year for the first time I revisited the church where I was married on June 21, 1947. It's a little church set away from the village on the brow of a hill. There were dark wooden box pews and oil lamps inside, slender blue harebells in the grass amongst the gravestones outside.

I have never belonged to any church, but I loved that church. It was like a dream come true going back home to be married there in that secret, cherished place.

Now nearly 50 years later, I found the door was open. I went inside. It was the same as I remembered—except for electric light and the now well polished wooden pews. Loving hands had cared for this little church all the intervening years.

"I was married here," I told the woman who was busy preparing the church for tomorrow's service. She fetched the old book from the Registry and we found the date. There were our signatures—Harold's and mine—it was a strange moment.

I didn't tell the woman how short a time our happiness had lasted, how soon that happiness had changed to disillusion and regret, that now he was dead—that husband to whom I had said so gladly "I will."

How estranged I felt from that past, as if I were witnessing another person's signature—not my own. I went outside into the sunny spring churchyard and asked myself—who was it who was married here nearly 50 years ago and signed her own name there for the last time?

It was like thinking of somebody else's past—as if the past I remembered so clearly didn't belong to me—as if it belonged to another person. No—my life hadn't lived up to those high expectations I had when I got married. I'd had to change.

I suppose even now—if I could change one thing in my life it might still be the fulfillment of that love's young dream, living happily into old age and for ever after with the man I'd married... except that he, or I, or we, would have had to be very different sorts of people.

Righteous Anger

I've been thinking a lot about things since I wrote that letter to Brenda and remembered the little church where I was married. I've been thinking it is one thing to adapt to changes in your life when YOU decide for yourself what those changes might be, or at least have an equal say. It's an entirely different matter when the changes that come are forced upon you, as they have been for Brenda—especially at this particular stage in her life when she was looking forward to a comfortable retirement.

Now I am hoping Brenda is feeling a goodly amount of righteous anger about how things have turned out for her and all the difficulties she is having to face up to. Some experts tell us that anger can be a strong and a positive motivator. And I agree with them!

Anger is what drove me—after I had been sacked (very unjustly!)—into taking a Social Science degree course at the new University of York in 1963, and it changed my life! I look back now and feel an odd sort of gratitude to the woman who said to me that morning out of the blue "We shan't be needing you any more after the holiday." I was devastated. And then I was angry.

"Rage! Rage!" I remembered Dylan Thomas's words to his father— "Rage, rage, against the dying of the light!" And over the years I've learned that we women have a right to our rage as well as men...we old women especially, otherwise we remain invisible, we agree to go quietly, to grow old gracefully, to get lost in self-pity.

Our anger doesn't have to be destructive or directed from spite. We don't necessarily have to fear or suppress it. We have to get it out—get it out to work FOR us.

And I'm thinking now that this is what Brenda needs to do—to get the anger out and acknowledge all those negative feelings of rejection, resentment and disappointment she has naturally experienced since her husband left and her life changed so drastically. Then to let the energy flow in a new direction, towards being the person Brenda wants to be, doing the things she really wants to do—for herself—all the things that will help to rebuild her sense of self-esteem. That's what I mean by the anger working for us—letting it push open new doors, being somewhere we've always wanted to be and maybe never dared, or had the opportunity, to be before.

Brenda's self-esteem will have taken a great knock since her husband left her. Nor have I forgotten that Brenda says in her letter that she's a lot less well off now than she hoped she would be in retirement. That makes a difference. It's no good denying it. Everything comes that much harder when money is short. It makes all the difference in the world to be able to go off on holiday or to be able to have a spending spree—even a small one. Just going out for a coffee or a bus trip into town may now have to be considered a rare treat. New ventures and hobbies, new friends and interests are bound to cost money.

So it is going to be harder. But read on, Brenda! There is a lot in the chapters which follow that I hope will give you a start in rebuilding your self-esteem and the courage to begin enjoying life again, perhaps more than you ever dared to hope when you first wrote your letter to the Hen Co-op.

Wedded Miss
Anne

I expected to live happily ever after. All the omens were favorable. But it did not work out like that. Our wedding photographs show a loving couple, heads inclined towards one another. We both have one weak eye muscle, and we both compensate for this minor disability by inclining our heads, mine to the right, his to the left. We have to make sure we are sitting or standing on the correct side of one another or it can look most unfriendly.

We both lived in the same London suburb, our parents were friends, there is one day difference in our ages. We didn't decide how we wanted our wedding to be. Our parents made all the decisions, and we went along with them because that was our expectation, and we didn't feel we had a choice. Very different from my son's recent wedding, where he and his wife wanted something different from the run-of-the-mill celebrations, and made sure they got it. When I compare the two sets of photos, I see us looking very proper and serious, posing stiffly with the background of a London hotel room. Then I look at theirs, some posed, but some spontaneous, gazing lovingly into each other's eyes, in front of a background of trees, lawns, a brass band, animals and model dinosaurs! What a contrast.

We made a comfortable home together, we had a boy and then a girl. What could go wrong with such a marriage? We had known one another for six years before we married while he completed his law exams and National Service. Time enough you would think to know each other, to discuss our future together, to develop a relationship that would meet the needs of us both. How naive we were, how hemmed in by the constraints of our upbringing.

What had started so full of hope on that sunny spring day in March 1955 ended. We separated, then divorced and began our lives apart.

We have both lived fulfilling lives since that parting fifteen years ago, and I hope we will continue to maintain the good friendship we now share. At our son's recent wedding we sat together at the top table, he with his wife on his other side.

Wedding celebrations may have changed along with the awareness and expectations of the bride and bridegroom, but one thing has not changed: many young people still expect the relationship to last until "death us do part."

We live so much longer, there are so many more strains and stresses in our lives. There is a big increase in the numbers of marriages which end in divorce. When divorce has not been our choice, the loss of the partner can be deep and time is needed to grieve for the serene old age we had expected with that person. After that, we have to rebuild our lives, make new beginnings, seek out old friends and make new ones.

> **Living in the past is a dull and lonely business,
> looking back strains the neck muscles, causes
> you to bump into people not going your way.**
> *Edna Ferber*

My Wedding Day
Barbara

Not long ago I was a guest at a wedding in what used to be called Marylebone Town Hall and my mind drifted back to the last time I had been inside that imposing edifice, 43 years ago…

…August 28, 1951. Our wedding day. I was all of twenty years old and I knew where I was going. I did not think of myself as a rebel, a breaker of moulds, but nevertheless I was the first in our extended family to marry "out"—to marry a non-Jew. I remembered the hushed whispers about acquaintances who had done so but these whispers did not seem to apply to me. This was no hole-and-corner affair, Julian was nearly 30, an architect, a man of substance, and he had chosen me. I was proud, happy and optimistic.

Some of the more orthodox members of my family boycotted the wedding but the ones I liked most were there at the register office for the brief ceremony. A few routine words and then the registrar said "place the ring on your wife's finger." His wife! I was now his wife! How amazing that my life would never be the same again because of those few words. I had no doubts at all. I knew that this marriage was right, that we loved each other and that nothing would ever change that.

We spent our honeymoon in Cornwall, in a fisherman's cottage on the cliffs above the little village of Cadgwith. We had a four-poster bed with curtains all around. It filled the tiny room. We had made love before we were married but we had never had the luxury of spending the night together and waking up together the next morning. This was bliss, crowned by the pleasure of hearing the fisherman's wife Mabel saying "What would you like for breakfast, Mrs Tayler?" Who? Me? Mrs. Tayler? That's who I was now, Mrs. Tayler forevermore.

Why did I so meekly accept, even welcome, the fracturing of my identity? It is hard to imagine a man being prepared to label himself as the property of his wife by giving up his own name and taking hers—so why do women agree to this mark of ownership? I applaud young women who have the self-confidence and strength of identity to retain their own names while still making a commitment to a relationship. I know that I was too unaware, too conditioned by social mores for the thought to even enter my head at the time. And now it feels too late. For despite the breakdown of our 20-year marriage, I was still Barbara Tayler, mother of the four Tayler offspring. I could not go back to the name of the young girl I had been; she was a different person, her name no longer meant anything to me. My adult identity was as Barbara Tayler forever-more.

It was my willing acceptance of this identity plus my confident assumption of the role of Mrs. Tayler that made it all the harder to deal with the painful feelings I suffered when our marriage ended. When my husband fell in love with another woman I was overwhelmed by feelings of rejection, anger and jealousy. Jealousy is a destructive emotion, corrosive and debilitating. My days and nights were soured by its effects. I lost all sense of my self-worth, all my self-esteem. But, with the help of loving friends, I began to realize that I was responsible for allowing my life to be destroyed by my jealousy and pain. It took time but in the end my self-image began to be rebuilt and I was able to move on. I realized that this is my life, the only one I've got, and nobody else could put it right for me. I began to look around with a degree of optimism, to make new friends and develop new interests which did not depend on being half of a couple. And now I can look back on my wedding day with equanimity and acknowledge that my life might not have turned out the way I expected but maybe it has turned out even better. In fact, my ex-husband recently expressed the view that I should be grateful to him for leaving!

My Career As a Model
Anne

My career as a model began when I was forty, in 1970! I have just come across the transparencies of myself which were intended for a poster to be displayed throughout London, advertising a Red Rover bus, which would run through the West End, picking up and dropping shoppers who visited the great London stores.

It all started in the Whitechapel Art Gallery, where, with a friend, I was enjoying some paintings by a then little-known artist called David Hockney. Suddenly a young woman came up to me and asked whether I would be willing to act as the model of a housewife on a shopping spree. After a few minutes' hesitation, I agreed. I allowed her to take a few snaps to show to the photographer to see whether I was suitable for this demanding project. Expecting that to be the end of the matter, we continued looking at paintings of pristine swimming pools in bright acrylic blues.

I was surprised when, a few weeks later, I was contacted and asked to go to an address off Tottenham Court Road. My friends were amazed at my good luck. Surely this was the start to a sensational career. My expectations were great.

Being a rather timid young matron in those days, I asked a friend to go with me. When the front door was opened by a large, scruffy young man, and I was ushered down a dark, narrow staircase to the basement, I was glad I was not alone. I had been asked to wear the emerald green suit and white sweater which I had been wearing when "spotted" in the gallery, and to bring a suitcase of other clothes which might be suitable for the photos. Armed with this, I entered the small studio.

Cameras, lights, screens were all set up in a businesslike manner. Wearing my green suit, I stood under the hot lights in anticipation of my splendid future, in this lucrative and prestigious career. I was handed carrier-bags and large parcels adorned with the logos of well-known stores, which were hung from my wrists and filled my arms. I felt like a Christmas tree with my multicolored appendages! The camera clicked away. My expectation that a model's work is easy and fun faded after about one-and-a-half hours, as my legs and arms ached and the heat became unbearable.

My reward for this session was a fee of twelve guineas, a very acceptable sum in those days, especially as my only source of income was the weekly housekeeping money. I treated myself and my faithful friend to an exotic meal at a restaurant in Hyde Park, and was still left with enough money for a taxi to the mainline station for our journey home.

Sadly, those photos were never used. Maybe they thought I didn't look right as Mrs. Average, the typical London shopper, after all. Now, many years later, in faded jeans, "Wild Women" T-shirt and unruly hair, I certainly would not fit the bill.

So that was the end of my modeling career. I never became a famous model with a face known to millions! But it was fun.

Needlework and Cookery
Barbara

Rummaging through the tea-chest under the stairs, the receptacle for all my life's odds and ends which have not found proper resting places, I came across a slim green book: "Swansea High School for Girls. Report Book. 1942-1945. Barbara Samson."

I flipped through the pages, glancing at each term's report. There were marks for the end-of-term exams and marks for the term's work. Marks over 60% were in red and those under 60% in black. What a model pupil I must have been! Column after column of cheerful red figures smiled up at me. Except—what's this? On each page, standing out from the pleasing reds, are two marks in black—Needlework and Cookery. I was hopeless at both. Every week on Cookery day I would carry to school my mother's shopping basket, containing the ingredients for the week's recipe, reluctantly spared from our meagre rations. And every week I would carry home the basket, with a clean cloth covering my latest sad product—soggy cakes or leathery pies. Needlework was no better. The apron, whose offensive hemstitching had to be unpicked again and again, never reached completion. My seams never lay flat, my stitches were uneven, my cloth was always grubby and spotted with blood from pricked fingers.

From school to university to marriage and motherhood I went and soon my days were filled with housewifely and motherly duties. Did I use my history, geography, physics? Not really. What I most needed were the skills I had disdained to acquire, the cookery and the needlework.

Of course I am not suggesting that the rest of my education was wasted. Far from it. But how irrelevant it seemed at that time, as I learned to care for my babies, bake bread, make cakes which were light and moist and produce pies with succulent, crumbly pastry, or to unpick an old coat to make it into a child's. I began to recognize what pleasure these tasks could bring and to value women's talents in juggling so many different skills in running a home, raising a family and often working outside the home too.

I do believe that, if I had to sit my end-of-term exams now, there might be a column of black marks indicating all the facts and theorems I have forgotten but there would be two red marks—for Cookery and Needlework.

On Being Single
Marie

There are many possible reasons for being a spinster, not simply that noone has ever asked you to marry them. There are many possible consequences too. This is my story.

At nineteen I found myself in London on the verge of a nervous breakdown, without a firm sense of identity or any confidence that I could cope with the pressures of life. A feeling of anguish grew more and more overwhelming until I felt suicide to be the only way out. No one seemed to be aware of my existence, let alone care. I survived because a couple took me in and cared for me.

Later I fell in love with a married man. I was a pure Anglican girl and he became the vicar of the church I attended. It was a long relationship during which I kept boyfriends at arm's length because of my hidden attachment. I had sexual feelings which he deliberately aroused but did not satisfy and I had a great longing for children of my own. As soon as opportunity presented itself I escaped to live elsewhere. But he had given me a ring not too obviously an eternity ring—which I wore for the next 20 years. Oh, the power of a ring! Such a little symbol, only a few millimeters across! It became a shackle. I finally divested myself of it both inwardly and outwardly when it was consigned to the Thames. But it did its work and kept me single.

Do I regret the single life? It has been something of a rollercoaster. There is a deep nest-making instinct in some women which can be an inner pressure, and so it was for me. A nest for one lacks something. At first I desperately wanted babies and was envious of the pram-pusher. Then I wanted little children. This craving was met over a period of time by teaching some 200 small children in a state school. Later I wanted lively adolescents going out into the world. Now I am old I see what pleasure—and pain—friends have in their families but the pressure is gone. Nature is finally merciful. I love my home. It doesn't need to express anyone's personality but mine. Nobody enters it who is not truly welcome. My home is my second skin. For a long time it felt unnatural to be single. I attended the weddings and christenings of my friends. They were excited and full of new hopes. Could there be a man for me? I know now that my repressed sexual feelings stole a great deal of my creative energy. I had lovers—not too many, not too few, one of them young. They were often fun, I cared for them a lot but marriage? No. I never found anyone else with whom I wanted to spend the rest of my life. Also, the positive value of independence became clearer and clearer. Married and encumbered friends were becoming envious in their turn. Such freedom! Nevertheless the desire for a male partner dies hard. And I was well into my forties before I really began to deal with the unresolved problems remaining from my childhood and the leftover feelings attached to that fatal ring and all it represented. It took me a long time to know who I really was and what I really wanted. I discovered what wonderful friends women are, so warm, supportive, interested and interesting, really good companions. I sometimes regret I am not a Lesbian. Would it have simplified matters? Having no permanent male partner has not interfered with my strong sense of gender. There's not a lot of lurking lust (though I still feel my sexuality and register who is fanciable!). I suspect, though, my singleness has been a way to preempt meeting the sort of pain I met before—perhaps it is a kind of cowardice.

So, for the past 20 years I have lived alone, with occasional visitors. I am a person who likes and needs to be alone a good deal. Solitude is not the same as loneliness. It is a positive state which enables me to make an inner journey, where I can loose myself from past conditioning. Here I find a newness that allows expansion and is the source of creativity which expresses itself in many ways. I have been lonely though. It usually strikes me after Christmas, when I return from celebrating in a home where three generations come and go. Energy seems not to flow when I return and I can feel depressed until my own life starts to move forward again. I usually have a Hen Party in January, which I suspect is other people's pit-of-the-year too. Loneliness is something you first learn in childhood and you are bound to meet it at some time or another. Later I belonged to a whole network of people with similar beliefs or interests—for example, lately making new connections through the Growing Old Disgracefully groups—and this for the most part has kept loneliness at bay.

So now I am 65. It's something of a joke. Can it really be true? The mirror says yes. Something warm and peaceful in me says yes too. I am much freer from the me I used to be and happier than I was when young. I am my own friend now and am not afraid to do what I feel like. (I have just joined a performing dance group.) It seems to me all this is probably because I have been single all these years. What seemed like misfortune was perhaps not so at all. I have been driven to stand on my own two feet, use my own judgment, search out my own inner meaning. Growing old is a happy process!

Don't Hold Your Breath
Maxine

Not long ago I read a book by Terry McMillan called *Waiting to Exhale*. The breath-holding metaphor started me thinking about how much of my own life was spent literally and figuratively waiting to exhale, waiting for the moment when I would be free to let go. There always seemed to be an expectation that everything would be all right if only...

When I grow up, then I'll be able to make my own rules and be who I want to be. But before I can relax, I must attract a mate, then wait for a proposal, then...

When I get married, I will be a fulfilled woman and live happily ever after.

When my husband is finished with his medical training, he'll be more available and we will be a happier family.

When the children are grown, life will be easier and I will have fewer responsibilities, then I will enjoy life more.

When I finish my courses and get a job, I will have spending money, then I'll relax and have fun.

When I lose weight I'll be OK, then I'll buy clothes that I enjoy wearing.

When, when, when. Always waiting, forgetting to breathe. Tapes playing in my head: Hold your stomach in; Keep your legs together; Never lose your temper; Be nice; Be lady-like; Don't be wild; Stop emoting; Never call attention to yourself. How could I breathe when I was holding so much in? And what did I gain by all the held breath, when reality never seemed to match my expectations?

With the illusions came the disillusions. For example, all the years of scrimping, hard work and energy I had put into the early years of my marriage, the fruits of which supposedly would be reaped when my husband became a successful physician, the waiting and dreaming of easier times to come, what happened to it all? As soon as we were at the point of being able to exhale, the marriage ended and my husband started a new family with someone else.

Now as I grow old disgracefully, I no longer wait for the future, preferring instead to concentrate on the present and what it has to offer me and what I have to offer it. Because if I have any regrets at all about my life, it would be that I missed so much along the way, failing to fully appreciate the present as it happened. This is not to say that there were no joyous occasions or happily remembered moments. It is just that I believe I was not fully participating in those moments because one part of me was always waiting to exhale.

> **Life is something that happens to you while you're making other plans.**
> *Margaret Millar*

Collectors' Pieces
Shirley

If I had to move my space
To some protected pensioners' place,
How could I bear to leave my things
My knick-knacks, pots and ruby rings
Collected over many years,
Memories which bring joy and tears?

How could I part with Uncle Maurice
Who haunts with his Renaissance face?
A poster once in London's tube
He smiled on me and all my brood.
A sort of talisman he became
So when divorced, my home divided,
I fought to keep him long and hard
That was what I then decided.

So when at last the time does come
And old age makes me choose,
He'll come again and I'll succumb
But also take my walking shoes,
My garlic press and Cumbrian pots,
My weaving frame and story plots,
My sloppy slippers and thick bright sweaters,
My typing paper and word processor,
My photos and the albums too
To put in place for you know who.

Such precious things make life worthwhile,
Keep me active, free to smile.
But things are things and their importance less
Than all the friends and thoughts and love,
    that I possess.

Betty

Expectations
Edith

I can't remember when or where it was that in the course of a book group discussion the question of "expectations" arose. I think it was Barbara who asked me, "Did you have expectations for your children?" No hesitation in my response, "Of course I did, isn't it natural?" I don't recall the actual substance of the ensuing conversation but it did make me think about my strong expectations for their future, although that didn't prevent them from doing the unexpected. It also set me wondering about myself and how had I foreseen the future when I was growing up. Since I was very much a product of my generation, first a college education, then marriage and a family would follow. I had no thoughts about "who" except I was anticipating a romantic attachment; nor did I think about the "where"; the "when" I trusted would be before I was 25. I had a definite expectation of a different life style from the deprived one in which I was growing up. While there were no clearcut ideas about it, I could easily picture myself in one of the glamorous interiors frequently seen on cinema screens in the early 1930s. It was difficult not to escape into that unreal movie world. Life for me and many of my friends was dreary and unrewarding; what a relief to spend a Saturday afternoon in the company of those more fortunate people who led such magical lives, dressed in those enchanting clothes and who married, living happily ever after. A world in which they never seemed to age and all things were possible.

I wouldn't have rejected that life style if it was offered, but I had no expectation that it would be, nor did I have any expectation of growing old. Within my family I had little contact with any ageing members. Our grandmother lived with us briefly when I was ten, but if I had thought about growing old at all, it would have had nothing to do with her.

Time has moved on, I with it. Friends and relations have died; I have seen my own husband physically deteriorate before me; yet I continue to distance myself from that process. Do I really believe I will always be able to swim, dance, jump a rope or even run for a bus should the need arise? I look for some of the answers in a game I have played with myself over the years. I began playing it when I was coming up to 50 and have continued with it from time to time. The object of the game is to see how I compare, at any given age, with my mother when she was at the same stage in her life. (She died at the age of 93.)

Now that I am 76, I try to picture her in 1965 when she was that age. I can see her living alone in her New York apartment, leading a very active life. Travelling on public transport, to the theatre with friends, or to play bridge, or to see the family; very much in charge of her own life. Then a flying visit to us in London during the summer, greatly enjoying her time here, but always keen to return to her own independent living arrangement. It's such a positive image of her that I can't imagine her being 76. Perhaps I'm saying something about myself now. My game moves ahead five years; she is 81, still to come for me. I take a peep into the crystal ball; the year is 1970. It's the year our son, Peter, was married in New York and the entire family went over for that special event. I find a photograph of her dancing with her son at the wedding, another shows her deep in conversation with a relative. Things don't seem to have altered in that five-year interval. Same activities, still public transport, the same lively interest in politics and world events as well as the yearly summer flights to London. She was, of course, still in her own apartment.

So long as my game continues to provide those positive images, I hold on to my ability to cope with the here and now. When those images begin to transmit other messages, I might need to adjust accordingly, but until that time, the aforementioned activities go on, although I'm not so sure about catching that bus.

Looking Back
Barbara

There was a time…
When our house was filled with voices—
Where's my pen? What time's supper?
Have you seen my…?
Did you know that…?
Laughing, squabbling,
Children and their friends.

There was a time…
When each day was a sharing,
Each evening time for talking,
We'd disagree, debate and argue,
Watch TV or listen to some music,
Sharing the experience.

Let's not romanticize.
It wasn't perfect.
But it was a family, my family.

And now I live alone
In my quiet peaceful tidy house.
Go out with friends
And come back alone
To this warm quiet house.
And mostly it feels fine
But sometimes I want to scream,
And sometimes, in the silence,
I hear my voice say aloud
"It wasn't meant to be like this."

The Seven Stages of Shirley Meredeen: Woman

Shirley

(with apologies to Shakespeare)

All the world's a stage
And all the men and women merely players:
They have their exits and their entrances;
And one woman in her time plays many parts,
Her acts being seven ages. At first the infant,
Dressed in pink, loved and allowed to cry.
Then the tomboyish schoolgirl with her satchel,
Pimples and pig-tails, skipping
Willingly to school. And then the teenager,
Adoring Fred Astaire and Bing,
Hidden in dark, sixpenny matinee seats
With shy longing for both romance and career
Yet heeding warnings of early pregnancy.
Then the working mother rushing
From job to home, from shop to parents' evening,
Panting for breath while maintaining strength and service
Within job and needy family. Weary, sometimes
Short of temper but loving always. Then the mid-age
Woman, secure in self-knowledge
Yet resisting separation from fledglings. Anxious as a
Mature student returned to singledom and solitude,
But finding herself. The sixth age shifts
Into the wise crone, with thickened body, greying hair,
Knowing that her time has come for fun.
When she can choose to play with grandchildren

Whose parents still rush in their turn
To feed, clothe, house their infants.
Last scene of all, in disgraceful serenity,
Having shed responsibilities
For others, having done her duty many times. Shrunk in body
But sans guilt at enjoying the fullness of a life
Of hard labor. Clear in head though perhaps not in memory,
Recognizing, with others, her wisdom, her life of service,
Her right to continued life, love and joy to the end.
Avec her own teeth, avec bespectacled eyes, avec
Appreciation of good taste in most things.
Avec almost everything.

If Only
Edith

Looking unhappiness straight in the face hasn't always helped me see myself through difficult periods, especially when I was growing up. Daydreaming was sometimes a satisfactory substitute. One of my favorite fantasies had its origins in my mother's family secret, revealed to us when I was in my early teens. It concerned her younger brother who had disappeared sometime before World War I. He had been an addictive gambler and had run away when his accumulated debt had become more than he could cope with. My daydreaming ran riot with that story. Always seated somewhere, either a park bench, a bus, or even the school library, I would be startled by a tap on my shoulder, then a query, "Are you Edith Halpern?" When I looked up to confirm this, there was this well-dressed, bearded gentleman explaining he was my long-lost uncle, now a wealthy man, offering to share his bonanza with me. There were other scenarios, always with a happy, magical ending, brought to that conclusion by a fairy godmother in various guises with the symbolic magic wand; a rescue package, a catalyst that would vastly improve my life.

That daydream fantasy world came to an end a long time ago although it hasn't prevented me reflecting on the past, wondering "if only." "If only" what? If I could have changed one thing, what would it have been? I look through my internal file of possibilities, eventually settling on education, and the time I spent at college, all seven years of it. The reality was a full-time job, classes at night, homework at the weekend, and little time for social life. This was hardly an ideal arrangement. Out-of-town college, living away from home, that's what I could have wished for. Freedom from parental restrictions, a whole, new inspiring environment plus all the trimmings that went with this new situation. College clothes for the Class of 1935, a wardrobe of my choosing, adequate for the social whirl, then very much a part of the college scene.

Better educational opportunities of course, but social ones too. With improved qualifications, perhaps even a postgraduate degree, there's no knowing where these different paths would have taken me. But, if my life had so changed, look what I would have missed: I would not have met and married Charles, nor come to England, nor had the children and grandchildren that followed, nor would I now be sitting at the typewriter trying to write. I want to keep this part of my life as it was and is.

So what one thing *would* I change? Well, if possible I would wipe out a small incident that occurred when I was about nine or ten years old. It might sound trivial but its effect has lasted up to the present day. It happened during a singing lesson when our music teacher told me I was not to sing in class or assembly ever again because I was singing out of tune (she said) and unable to pitch my voice properly. I was now and forever branded "a listener," deprived of the pleasure of group singing.

Nowadays children are encouraged to sing, not denied that pleasure. And courses are being offered to help people overcome this problem. I have just heard about such a one that is at present taking place at The Mary Ward Centre (a London Adult Education Center), entitled "Singing for the Tone Deaf". Who says there are no fairy godmothers?

CHAPTER TWO
Do I Still Have Choices?

Dear Hen Co-op,

When I read your book I thought what lucky women you are. You seem able to retire, take holidays, travel and do exciting things. I don't have choices like that. I have to continue my job although I'm nearly 69 because I know that it's going to be difficult to manage on my pension. I live in a small house with my husband who doesn't want to go out or do anything and doesn't want me to do anything either. I just don't have the choice of growing old disgracefully. Can you help me?

Yours in need,

Joan

Dear Joan,

When as older women we begin to take stock of our lives, it often seems that our choices are narrowing, that we are less able to get past the burdens that seem to be holding us back. Some restrictions, such as declining health or financial circumstances, are very real; others may be ones we stay with because they are familiar. But that is also a kind of choice, to do nothing about the things we can change.

In the past you made choices that led you to your present situation. Some of those choices involved risk-taking and conscious decision making. Others may have been made because you had been conditioned to think of them as your only options, when in fact there were alternatives. As we age, some of our choices may become restricted and we may have more limitations, but we can still create new choices within our circumstances.

Those of us in the Hen Co-op acknowledge that we are blessed with reasonably good health, supportive families and friends, and while not princely incomes, enough money to allow us to have the occasional treat or holiday. We know the situation for some people presents less flexibility, such as Irene points out in her piece on living in an old-age ghetto. However, we also hear from many women who are finding that their choices are not as limited as they thought.

The first step is to decide realistically what you can and cannot do. For example, you say you cannot quit work because your pension would be too small. Women in the Growing Old Disgracefully Network are writing to tell us that even on a small pension there are many things they can do together that are fun but cost very little money. Walking, talking, circle dancing, attending lectures, singing, picnics—the list is endless. The key is finding other women who enjoy some of the same things you do, and the activities will follow. Admittedly, for those who are single, it is easier, but married women are discovering that they, too, can choose to change their lives.

You say that your husband does not want to go out to do things so you are stuck at home. Why? Just because he is a grumpy old bore doesn't mean that you have to turn into one as well. He may not want to change, but remind him that you did not marry a grumpy old bore and you do not want one for a husband now. Instead of adjusting to his lifestyle, you could decide to go on and do things alone or with other women. If you start thinking in terms of how much better your relationship could be if you were happy and had new things to talk about, you may decide that you can come out from under all the "shoulds" and "oughts" you have been burdened with, and start letting yourself shine through. In the end you will be doing everyone a favor.

As individuals and as the Hen Co-op, the six of us have taken risks to get us to this point. We had to let go of lifelong ways of thinking and reexamine our relationships with family, friends and coworkers. There are new challenges daily, and things we don't get right, but each of us helps the others to come up with creative solutions. As we stressed in our first book, trying to grow old disgracefully on your own is a formidable task. The odds may overwhelm you. A supportive network can make the difference in how well you stand up to the pressures on you.

It is tempting to play the game of "If it weren't for you I could…" but in fact, you *can* make your own choices. Barbara points this out with good humor in her "Scene with Three Endings": Is it really someone else who is holding you back? What do you fear might happen if you assert your intention to grow old disgracefully? As author Erica Jong says, "The trouble is, if you don't risk anything, you risk even more."

Sure, your husband might be put off, but then, isn't it up to him to examine why he has a hard time considering your needs? Just because it's always been that way is not a good reason for letting it go on. Staying with a familiar pattern and not taking risks is your choice, but if you want a change, start by taking small steps, try something new a little bit at a time. If you do this each day, you may find that you develop enough confidence to take bigger strides, and before you know it you will be growing old as disgracefully as you like.

Yes, our options do become different as we age. But they are not gone. As Maxine says, "You can choose to have the blues". So evaluate which restrictions are real, and which you are placing on yourself out of fear or inertia. Nobody wants to end his or her life regretting what could have been if only… This won't happen to you if you start now to take charge of your own life. A creative attitude won't take away the realities of your circumstances, but it will help you open your mind to options you may not have considered.

Disgracefully yours,

The Hen Co-op

Choices
Barbara

We make choices every day, most of them trivial—what do I fancy for supper or what shall I wear today? Then there are other more significant choices—can I afford a holiday this year or should I save for repairing the roof? Then above and beyond those are the real life-changing choices about jobs, marriage or other partnerships, moving to another house or moving to a new town or country. These decisions are all within our own choice and yet, when you look back over your life do you have the feeling that for most of the time you were swept along by an inexorable tide? Do you find it impossible to remember the moments when you actually made a choice?

I remember the powerlessness of childhood as I was moved from house to house, from school to school and was never asked what I felt about the changes. As I grew older, I suppose I did have choices when it came to leaving school and going on to further education but, looking back, it seems that I took the first option with little awareness or consideration of alternatives. And then my biological urges kicked in and I found myself falling in love. Of course it was not just the biological urges but also the effects of the romantic soup in which we all swam at that time. The Hollywood films, the schmaltzy popular songs—eyes meeting across a crowded room—the touch of his lips—falling in love with love. Being in love can be so dangerously blinding—it befuddles your judgment and is probably the worst time for making decisions. Like chicken pox, it runs its course and passes, leaving its scars and, if you are lucky, it is replaced by love, which is a very different kettle of fish. So, at 19, I didn't even hesitate when Julian asked me to marry him. The biggest, most significant choice of my life and I said yes, just like that—and there I was, married at 20, and a series of nonchoices followed, moves around the country as Julian rose up the job ladder, then babies, one, two and three in rapid succession. I suppose we did discuss the pros and cons but I had no separate existence to add to the equation.

Then, back in London (yet another job-move for Julian), when our youngest was three, I was offered a part-time job and, for the first time it seemed, I made a significant choice for myself. It was a job which took me out of the home, even if for only two hours a day. It led to new interests and new friendships and it changed my life. Some years later along came baby number four. I have to admit that this was not initially by choice but by accident, the sweetest, happiest *accident* of my life. But of course, there was a choice in proceeding when I realized I was pregnant, so yes, it was a positive choice after all.

When my marriage foundered a few years later I felt driven by events beyond my control. If I did have a choice I was not aware of it at the time, though looking back after so many years I can see that I could have chosen to act differently—but that is with hindsight.

How different things are now. I am in control of my own life. I can choose both the small things and the major ones. When to go to bed, when to get up, where to go, whom to see, where to live, where to go on holiday, what to do with the rest of my life. This is not to say that there are no constraints, I have to consider money, energy, health, family commitments and other obligations, but within those limits I hold my life in my own arms and make my own choices. Sometimes that freedom is frightening, even overwhelming, sometimes it is exhilarating. I don't know whether I always have a choice between those options but whenever I can I choose exhilaration.

> **I have yet to hear a man ask for advice on how to combine marriage and a career.**
> *Gloria Steinem*

Where Will I Live?
Anne

Where will I live when I'm ninety?
When my legs cannot climb up the stairs
When my eyes have become pale and rheumy
And my hearing is causing despair.
Will it be in a house shared with others?
Will it be in a home by the sea?
Or a flat with a warden to notice
When I can't get my dinner or tea?

Where will I live when I'm ninety?
Will it be on the edge of a cliff?
I can't worry about that at the moment
Although I am getting quite stiff.
I don't want to leave where I'm living
I don't choose to consider my fate,
So I'll leave it for now and not worry
Although I can't leave it too late.

Will God let me have ample warning
Perhaps she could give me a date
When a choice must be made for the future
Before I'm in too bad a state!

One Step At a Time
Mary

It's the politicians who talk about choice! In real life for most people most of the time choices are extremely limited.

Having a choice for me would mean knowing what the alternatives were and the likely consequences, as well as having the means to put my choices into effect.

In the past, like many other women of my generation, I think I was driven by the need to be like everybody else, to conform to society's expectations of what being female meant, to be chosen, to be loved, to be seen as desirable, to assuage self-doubt…

Looking back feels more like recalling a process than identifying the point at which I made a choice. Take for example my decision to marry my husband. There were weeks of panic and anxiety because I'd missed two periods and there were no abortion facilities around that I knew about. He offered me a ring…It was settled. But was it ever a choice?

My mother said "You'll get the rough end of the stick!" And she was right. And I'd asked for it, yes, I'd asked for it…But was it a choice? If it was, it belongs to a past self I don't want to own…that's the truth of it.

Dennis Potter said in his last interview just before he died that we should look back at our younger selves with unflinching honesty—and with tenderness. So that's what I need—honesty and tenderness—both.

Was the time when I left my husband a choice after over 30 years of marriage and when he was far from well? He'd always had asthma and it could only get worse. It's a time that's hard to write about, harder than any other time, because I suppose I have to own up to a lot of guilt about leaving him. And it would be a long story to tell because it goes such a long way back.

I'd always said to myself, from the early days of our marriage, though not to him or to anyone else, that I would leave when the children were old enough to be independent. He needed someone to look after him but I said to myself: "It does not have to be me. He does not mind who it is as long as there is someone 24 hours a day."

It was hard to go. But I cannot regret it. It never felt like making a choice. More like coming to the end of a long and painful journey—painful for both of us—painful to remember still.

Now I must think in the same way about what choices remain for me in the future. There is a hard choice waiting. It's one a lot of readers will recognize. It's this: how long can I stay here in this house—living on my own and 100 miles from the nearest member of my family? While I have good health it makes sense to stay where I am, doesn't it? I'm not a bother to any of them—not yet. I think this must be the very hardest choice of all—the choice to give up your own home. None of us wants to, not enough to make the fantasy of the old women's commune a reality anyway!

I remember so well when my mother had to give up her home—only 10 years ago. She was quite a lot older than I am now—she was 88, I think. I lived 50-60 miles away and I was still working full time.

I'd lived closer to her for many years previously. She'd helped me then while I was at the university and the girls were at school. She had them all for dinners and their Dad too—because they preferred her good cooking to school dinners and eating out!

I visited her evenings and weekends. I told her what I was learning in economics. She would have loved to have had that opportunity! And I bet she'd have got a first! But when it came to it, some years later, that she couldn't manage on her own any longer, I didn't want to have to ask her to come and live with me.

Instead she went to live with my sister and her husband 200 miles away. I helped her move and my heart ached for her. She was leaving the home I knew she loved so much. Just as I love mine now.

I remember the day she left her house for the last time. I took her hand as we went down the stairs and held it for a moment to give her all the comfort I could. It was too hard to find words—so I held her hand. Then she went outside to the car that was waiting for her—waiting to take her away forever. So courageous she was and circumspect—determined not to allow herself to be upset because it would have upset everyone else and made the leaving that much harder to bear.

So now—what of my own choice? I'm made of softer stuff than my mother was. I try again to imagine myself leaving this house, to see myself like my mother walking bravely out of the gate for the last time—and I fail!

Be tender with yourself—honest but tender...

And is that all there is to say—for the moment anyway? Can I put off making choices again for the time being? It's a *process*, I said just now. I'm only 70!

I can take one step at a time.

> **I used to dread getting older because I thought I would not be able to do all the things I wanted to do, but now that I am older I find that I don't want to do them.**
> *Nancy, Lady Astor*

Living
Barbara

We mark our lives with signposts
And move towards them day by day;
And then, each one achieved
Is seen to be another starting point.

Between yesterday and tomorrow,
This moment present, here and now,
Is but a pinpoint, a flicker.
And each most pressing need
Will join the other yesterdays, receding.

All our yesterdays are a series
Whose sum is today. Is that all?
Do we create trivialities to fill the time,
To give our little lives a sense of purpose?

We cannot face the stark reality
That the question "Why?" cannot be answered.
That glimmer of awareness some call soul,
Our unique intelligence, seeks to make sense of chaos.

But the only sense is in the living.
We ourselves can choose to open up our minds
To all that life can give, the only sense
Is in our own ability to make the most of life.

Mirage
Shirley

Being upwardly mobile has its downsides as well as its successes. As half of a marriage in which professional ambition played a large part, I spent much of our shared life working the ladder of company wife alongside my own work as a local journalist, together with prime responsibility as parent of two lively lads. Social friendships were largely superficial as we advanced from one job and home to another, leaving little time for deep relationships.

From choice, we had escaped from the family network which had strangled us prior to marriage. The loss of the quality of that deep intimacy—once resented—deepened the degree of exclusive reliance on each other. Had we wanted help from the family, our pride would have prevented admitting such a need. We had changed too, with a fresh attitude to life. We had escaped from a life of family-knows-best and narrow inflexibility, to another where new challenges were there to be grasped and habitual barriers were ignored.

So, after 20 years of what had seemed like a solid, happy marriage, when I began to have doubts about the quality and direction of my life in a two-adult-two-child unit, and in relation to the jobs I had done so far, I had to go inwards to work out solutions for the future.

It was hard to admit to the superficial gloss of those relationships born of success. It was hard to tell the family that my marriage was becoming daily more miserable and that he was having extramarital relationships. His pace of life—behind which I had breathlessly raced for so long—was really something I no longer enjoyed and the veneer of happiness was fragile. To tell my parents, who had felt abandoned when we moved first 200 miles north and later 200 west to escape them—and in their terms deny them their grandchildren—that it had all been a big mistake, was something I was not strong enough to share with them.

What had started as frustration soon turned to despair and then to rage. My self-imposed loneliness had rebounded on me. What seemed like a choice had become a penance. While I tried to come to terms with what I soon recognized as marriage failure and life-choice mistakes, my feelings turned to anger, spitefulness, then resignation. I became bitter and tearful, dreading the dawning of each day, going through the mechanics of daily routines.

Sometimes I avoided the pain with pretense and, at other times, I faced up to it with fierce quarrels. Was it possible to look away from his transgressions or attempt to unravel my own failings to improve our relationship? My friends had their own problems. No way could I tell the family nor would I have welcomed their advice. My own parents, whose marriage was disastrous but who had stuck it out, provided no useful precedent with their view of any marriage being better than divorce. I had no one to turn to and the pendulum swung daily between the choice of staying in an unhappy marriage or resignation to the finality of separation. My pillow was wet with tears both night and morning. My face wore an expression of hardness. I forgot almost how to laugh. The children's needs kept some semblance of humanity within the equation.

Our marriage had started and endured for some time with such strong interdependence. Our abandonment of our roots, our self-confidence in the route to happiness and success, had a heavy investment in its future. We dared not admit to failure to each other, let alone others. We had tried to be all things to each other, thinking that other relationships could not be as all-consumingly deep as ours. When we had exhausted those feelings there was an aching gap—much like those women who, having invested all their love, energy and time into their partners or children, suddenly feel lost when the partner dies or the children leave the roost.

That void of loss closed only when we finally admitted defeat in the marriage and started to move forwards on another plane—apart. Divorce released me from that insecure intimacy and I was free to start living again, to learn to trust others, make new qualitative friendships and to look back on that loneliness of those terrible last years within the marriage as a thing of the past.

Choosin' the Blues
Maxine

You can choose to have the blues,
stay to take what may
present itself. Cringe from
disapproval. Hate the moment, hate
to think of what comes next. OR
You can choose.

You can choose to have the blues.
Find a reason or two or three
to keep your feet
firmly in place. "If it weren't for you
I could have…" OR
You can choose.

You can choose to have the blues,
turn dreaming into stone,
make the tea, choke on the tea
that shuts the throat
So no screams scream. OR
You can choose.

You can choose to have the blues OR
You can choose.

Marion

A Scene With Three Endings
Barbara

Are you married to an old grouch? Does the master of your house take you for granted? Then read on…

The scene is a comfortable sitting room. The style is modern but not trendy, the armchairs deep and soft, the coffee table covered with newspapers and magazines. A fire burns in the grate and before the fire, legs outstretched, face buried in a newspaper, sits the Master of the House.

    Enter the Wife, bearing a tray loaded with a coffee pot, milk, sugar, cups and a home-made cake. She eyes the cluttered table.

WIFE: Darling, could you make some room on the table?

MASTER: *(without lowering paper)* Hmph.

WIFE: *(slightly louder)* Would you mind clearing a space?

MASTER: *(angrily lowering paper)* No need to shout. I heard you the first time.

He shoves a pile of papers aside and some fall to the floor. Wife sets down the tray, picks up the fallen papers and straightens the magazines. She sets out the cups and pours the coffee.

WIFE: Would you like some cake with your coffee?

MASTER: *(without lowering paper)* Mm.

Wife cuts some cake and places the coffee and cake on the table. She sits in the opposite chair with her cup of coffee and gazes into the fire. There is a long silence broken only by the clink of cups and the smacking of lips as the Master eats his cake.

WIFE: I made the cake this afternoon after I'd fetched the kids from school and taken the cat to the vet and called in with your mother's shopping.

MASTER *(without lowering paper)* Hm.

He reaches out and takes another bite of cake.

WIFE: Her leg is still in plaster so she can't really manage yet.

MASTER: *(without lowering paper)* Hm.

He finishes his slice of cake.

WIFE: My mother phoned this morning. She had a burst pipe so I had to call the plumber and rush round there to let him in.

Master does not reply. Is he asleep behind his newspaper? But no, he holds out his plate for more cake. Wife cuts another large slice and silently places it on his plate.
　　　Silence descends once more. Wife gazes into the fire. Master turns a page of his paper with much shaking and smoothing. He eats some more cake and holds out his cup for more coffee.

Now Choose Your Ending

1. The Mouse
Wife fills up his cup, he grunts and carries on reading. With a sigh she picks up her knitting.

2. The Tiger
Wife fills up his cup and leans back in her chair with a smug smile.

TIGER: I'm so glad you enjoyed the cake, my darling. I made it specially for you. You see, it's got a secret ingredient—arsenic.

MASTER: Argh...

3. The Disgraceful Woman

There is no response from the Wife. After a moment the Master peers round his paper. Her chair is empty but there is a note on the seat. Puzzled, he puts down his paper and picks up the note. It says:

I'm off to a meeting of my new women's group—it's called Growing Old Disgracefully and I think it's about time I did. Don't wait up. I'll probably be very late.

Staying Put
Edith

I am sure there must have been times when I was guilty of thinking I knew better how to order people's lives than they did; whether it was friends, relations, my husband or especially my children. It was either for "their own good" or just because "I knew best." So it was when my mother, then in her early eighties, decided she wanted to change her apartment in New York. Since it was rented, it was only necessary for her to find another apartment before her lease expired and to notify the landlord accordingly. When she first told us about her decision, we were delighted as there now seemed a possibility that she might locate closer to the center of the city. This seemed the ideal opportunity for her to be nearer to where both my sister and brother lived. Her current apartment was a long way from either of them. I, living three thousand miles away, was less involved, but kept informed, generally concurring with their recommendations and suggestions of suitable apartments that would have made visiting easier for my mother as well as for them. The other alternative was a Residential Home of which there were several good ones, well located. No amount of reasoning, persuasion or even a bit of bribery was of any avail. She was determined to keep control of her own life. When eventually she found an apartment, it was even further out of the city than the one she was leaving. She claimed she would be happier there than in any of the places her children had chosen for her. I know at the time we thought she was unreasonable, and she was, but we had to respect her decision.

I think about it now, not that my situation in any way mirrors hers but the memory of it was triggered when people began to ask me questions about my future living arrangements. It wasn't long after my husband's death, when in the course of conversation with friends or relations, the issue would arise. "Are you going to stay on in your flat, now that you are on your own?" occasionally adding, "Isn't it too large for one person?" or "Do you really want to go on living there NOW?" or perhaps a more subtle approach, "Don't you think it would be a good idea to move to Devon, nearer your family?"

Despite my husband's protracted illness, I managed to hold on to a portion of independent living. I am known and know people in the community. I like living where I am now; so many happy memories flow from here. Move to Devon to be nearer my children? Certainly not! This is no solution for me, especially having taken on board the Growing Old Disgracefully philosophy. Visit of course, and enjoy it all the more because I have my own space and life to return to. I am aware there may be a time when I am no longer able to maintain my flat or my independence; alternative living arrangements will need to be considered. I trust I will not be as intractable as my mother before me, but until then, I know who I am and I know where I shall be living. It is *my* choice.

Grumpy Old Bore
Shirley

I'm fed up.
He's content.

I want to read.
He wants TV.

I'd like to see the new film.
He'd rather watch football.

I need some exercise.
He wants to read.

I suggest an Indian takeaway.
He wants shepherd's pie.

"Let's go shopping", I say.
He wants to stay home.

Shall we go for a ride in the country?
It's going to rain.

Let's go to France for a holiday.
What's wrong with Bognor again?

I wear a new dress.
He doesn't notice.

I like kicking the autumn leaves.
"Don't be so childish," says he.

Do you like my new hairdo?
What was wrong with the old one?

Let's dance the samba.
I only know how to foxtrot.

Make me some toast, I request.
What's wrong with the bread, he snaps.

It's your turn to do the breakfast dishes.
Why not leave them till tonight?

Are you listening behind that paper?
Of course I am.

I'm fed up and I'm going to leave you.
What's wrong, he queries.

A Voice From the Ghetto

Irene

I did not know, until I picked up a copy of our local paper and began idly flicking through it, that I lived in a "ghetto for wrinklies." The words were those of a journalist comparing our warden-controlled Council bungalows with some new private retirement homes proposed at a holiday chalet park.

It is true that our bungalows would compare unfavorably with newly built and expensive privately owned accommodation. My own bungalow dates from about 1960 when the estate was built and reflects the general picture of old people in the minds of the architects and planners of that time. It is extremely small—the living room, bedroom, kitchen and bathroom would probably all fit easily into one room of a house owned by an architect or planner. It is obvious that it was designed by someone—a man almost certainly—who never actually envisaged a real live pensioner living in it, only a stereotypical old woman (a man was less likely to have survived), already grown old gracefully, content to sit in front of the fire (well, maybe the television) and knit. She would, being a Council tenant, belong to the lower orders and not have much furniture or kitchen equipment. So the accommodation would not have to include space for such things as musical instruments, phonographs and records, typewriters, sewing machines, books, trunks, suitcases, bicycles, shopping carts, extra bed linen, blankets, heavy coats, Wellington boots, umbrellas, garden chairs, lawn mowers, spades, forks and rakes, birdcages or dogs larger than Chihuahuas. Because of this failure of imagination or observation, our bungalows have the absolute minimum of cupboards, and no storage space outside, although each of us is supposed to look after our own patch of garden. The words "Wherever can I put it?" are never far from my lips—talking to myself, as I often do. On moving in, it was clear that the kitchen had not been designed to take a stove, fridge and washing machine, but only two of the three. In the end I sold my stove for $30 and kept the other two items because a kind friend gave me a microwave. Later I acquired a small tabletop oven and an electric hot plate and could cook anything with these. I might even have invited some people to a meal if there had been room for them to sit round the table. All this equipment meant an acute shortage of electrical outlets. The anonymous They had only allowed one per room and a double in the kitchen, so I had extension cords festooned all over the place, for the TV, radio, kettle, lamps, electric spaceheater and so on. Last year they rewired the whole estate and we got some more sockets but there still don't seem to be enough. It seems that the older you get and the less active you are, the more electrical gadgets you make use of.

Other things that the hypothetical occupant of one of these bungalows was not supposed to have included any family or friends outside the immediate neighborhood. Nobody could be invited to stay because of the lack of a spare room. It is true that many of the tenants here have children and grandchildren living near enough to pop in at teatime or to help with odd jobs such as shopping or cutting the grass but I have nobody within a hundred miles and there must be others in the same position. My next-door neighbor has provided herself with a convertible sofa-bed but I have never understood how she makes room for it. In any case my savings would not run to this expense. Nevertheless I have considered the matter and decided that the only item I could get rid of to make more space is the wooden chest in which I store spare bedding and towels. I might then beg, borrow or steal some sort of folding bed. But…if I dispense with the chest I would have nowhere to put the spare bedding and then there would be no bedding for the proposed spare bed—which would, in any case, occupy all the available space in the living room. And my state of health is such that I usually have to creep through the room on my way to the bathroom at least once a night, often more, taking great care not to step in the wrong place or knock anything over.

There is no end to the complications not envisaged by the architects who designed this retirement housing. My GP says I shouldn't complain. "It was an award-winning scheme at the time, you know. In those days lots of authorities were putting old people into tower blocks." In fact I don't complain all that much, except by way of repeated applications to the Council for a transfer to a two-bedroomed unit—something I was told would be easy. There are plenty of these as, in 1973, the Housing Department recognized that everybody needs a spare room and has not built any single-bedroomed places since. It seems, however, that there is no hope of a transfer for me. Whenever a bigger bungalow becomes available they find a couple of pensioners occupying an ordinary Council house and move them to sheltered accommodation, thus freeing a house for a family on the housing list. One can hardly blame the Council for this as the present Government has not allowed them to build any new Council houses. It certainly feels like a lunatic world and all a poor wrinkly can do is to carry on as disgracefully as possible in the so-called ghetto and hang on tight to her sanity.

The Power to Name
Maxine

For the first 24 years of my life, I carried my father's surname. Growing up in Texas with a name like Rachofsky presented problems; non-Jewish Texans (the dominant majority) found it hard to pronounce and even harder to spell. It was a great relief to me when I married a man whose name was White. It was short, simple, easy to say and hear, and fairly common.

My father's brothers had changed their name, shortened it to "Ray" for business purposes, or so they said. Daddy preferred to keep the family name, no matter how it got mangled in pronunciation, therefore it became my name automatically. I had no choice in the matter. Although I now appreciate his decision, at the time I didn't understand why anyone would not want to blend into the mainstream.

My husband's name was not the name his family came with to America. Like many other immigrants, their name became anglicized, either by choice or by someone else's decision, so Weisman became White. Roots were erased and origins negated by the act of renaming.

More than 20 years after I was divorced, I was still using the name White. At first I never even considered changing it, since my generation of women had never heard of such an option. Even when I began meeting other divorced women who were taking back their birth names, I thought that it would be confusing to have a different name from my children's. I now wonder if the real reason was a fear of being labeled as someone without a link to a man.

As I became more and more woman-identified, and my children were grown with families of their own, the idea of carrying around a name of a man just because I was once married to him seemed incongruous. To take back my father's name didn't seem right either. I could have chosen any name or created one, but instead I decided to use my mother's family name. I knew full well that she had been assigned her own father's name, but somehow it made me feel more connected to her and reminded me of the generative power of women. Also, my mother's brother was about to celebrate his 80th birthday. He and I have always been very close so I wanted to take their family name as a birthday tribute.

It was not an easy project to get a surname changed. Every license, credit card, insurance policy, employment record, subscription membership, correspondent had to be notified. Each place had its own rules for allowing a name change. Most often the question was, "Did you get married or divorced?" It seemed incomprehensible that someone would simply want to name herself differently. I had to produce signed affidavits allowing that Maxine Myers was the same person as Maxine White. I had to swear that I was not trying to avoid debts or criminal charges. I had to give a reason, and marriage or divorce seemed the only available, acceptable options for a woman.

After butting my head against bureaucracy for a while, I finally settled for saying, yes, I got a divorce, which, of course was true if you didn't care about when. I produced divorce papers from 1969; everyone was satisfied. It was then that I fully understood how much our society cares about marital status for women.

Changing my name is one of the most empowering things I've done for myself. I feel as if I finally have chosen my own identity, and though I took a family name, the act of choosing is what is important. Maxine Myers feels right, it fits me, it lets me create who I want to be. There is power in being the one to name, the one who is the active subject. The men who composed the Bible knew this when they assigned the act of naming to a male supreme being.

I doubt very much that I will ever want to change my name again, but if I do, it will be for my own reasons, and of my own volition.

CHAPTER THREE

What About My Sex Life?

Dear Hens,

I'm sixty-four years old and have been without a partner for a number of years. I find myself increasingly missing the companionship as well as the sex. While I do enjoy going out with friends from time to time, it's not sufficiently satisfying. I would like to experience again the intimacy of a relationship which would naturally include a sexual aspect. Have you any suggestions as to what options I can pursue and how I can go about accomplishing them?

Yours,

Miriam

Dear Miriam,

Most of us who are now in our sixties or older grew up in an age when women were not supposed to talk about sexuality, or admit to sexual feelings, especially not in public. We were most likely taught that our womanly bodies were not something to be proud of and that we should try as much as possible to conceal any evidence of natural bodily functions (see Anne's "The Shapely Pad").

The common myths of our youth were that women did not, maybe even could not, enjoy sex as much as men; that only men could be the initiators of physical contact; and that after a certain age, sex and physical intimacy became a thing of the past. Thanks to research and to the efforts of many brave souls in the Women's Movement, we know now that none of these myths is true; however, it is still the case, statistically speaking, that women live longer than men, and heterosexual women are often left without a partner with whom to express their needs for sex and intimacy.

Of course, not all women want to begin new relationships, sexual or otherwise. For them, there is a great relief in celibacy, as Mary says in "Shall I Never Be Desirable Again?" Because women in our society are judged desirable on the basis of youth and appearance, it seems that the older one gets, the harder it becomes to find new ways to satisfy our needs. But as Mary also shows, older women are beginning to open their thinking to include choices about how and with whom they want to be intimate, and to exercise those choices in a number of ways they may not have previously considered. Even though most women still think of sex in terms of a relationship with a man, sexuality can be part of our lives in many other ways.

In our group, we have had many discussions on the subject of masturbation. To pleasure yourself sexually may not bring the closeness to another person that you want, but it does provide physical release and gives you a chance to connect with yourself on an intimate level. It also keeps the equipment in running order, in the event that a partner should come along. And it is not just for the single woman; sometimes there are reasons why sexual needs are not met in a relationship, and, as Edith says, you cherish the moments of closeness and find sensual comfort with each other without having intercourse.

Throughout our lives we have probably had close emotional ties to other women, and these may become even more intense as we age. Some of us have chosen women as sexual partners all along, others of us are finding that even in old age, we can become intimate with women for the first time. There may even be some hormonal changes after menopause that contribute to an increased attraction to other women. Because heterosexual men often find much younger women for new relationships, the availability factor may also have an influence. Even when no sex is involved, some women are enjoying living together and finding a kind of intimacy that is sensually satisfying.

Being sensual with another person, with or without sex, requires a level of acceptance of one's body, and as older women, we may have a lot of negative feelings about our bodies. We may be struggling with physical changes that are occurring normally, or finding, as Maxine did, that illness is altering our bodies. In our culture, we rarely see older women's bodies celebrated, except for an occasional celebrity who has had innumerable hair colorings, face-lifts, tummy tucks, buttock pick-me-uppers, eyelid push-ups, silicone breast implants and lip enhancement. Any natural body thickening is seen as a moral flaw, and the normal aging process gets hidden and denied. It is no wonder that so many of us have trouble accepting that our old bodies can be a source of sensuality, but as the "Sex after Sixty" piece shows, new pleasures are not out of the realm of possibility.

There is no easy answer to the question of how and where to find new partners, if that is what you decide is best for you. Barbara describes her experience with placing an advertisement in the Lonely Hearts column, and while the results were not what she hoped for, other people have had success with this means of meeting someone. Or you can go on and pursue your own interests and find activities that are enjoyable, and if you meet someone else in these places, then at least you know you have a common interest on which to build a friendship, and you will have had a good time in the process. If the connection leads to a sexual relationship, assuming that is what you want, so much the better.

There is no reason not to enjoy sex and intimacy for as long as you live, despite cultural messages to the contrary. If you have had unsatisfactory experiences with sex in the past, or feel you have had enough and want to use your energy elsewhere, you may be happy to be celibate, at least for now, as Shirley says. Or you may find that it is really touching, hugging and physical contact that you want, and that you can find that with close friends.

The options we have mentioned and that we talk about in this chapter are not the only ones. As always, only you know what is right for yourself and your own situation. We wish you the best.

Disgracefully yours,

The Hen Co-op

Flying Virgin
Anne

This summer I flew for the first time with Virgin Atlantic. As I sat comfortably in my seat (does it have more leg-room than other airlines?) I was amused to read V.I.R.G.I.N. in large letters on the pull-down tray in front of me, on the fabric of the seats and on the little red bag of goodies with which this airline rewards its passengers.

I felt so labeled myself and remembered a conversation which we had had in the Hen Co-op in which we each told whether we were in this pure state when we married. Four answered "no" without a blush; I was one of the two who answered "yes" and I recalled the time when I guarded my virginity fiercely and would not have given it up whatever the temptation. Hadn't I been brought up to know that "nice girls didn't" and I was nothing if not a nice girl. I remembered the shock of excitement and horror I had felt in early courtship when "he" had touched my breast (through my clothes, of course!) I had felt that wanton touch with delight for days or weeks after. I was about nineteen, naive and passive, but I knew what could happen if I let things go any further.

My friends in those days were equally innocent. We knew we might have babies if we were not careful, we knew our value with *virgo intacta*. We were saving ourselves for our husbands on our wedding day and nothing would have induced us to break these unwritten rules.

When one of my friends got married before me, I can remember speaking to her on the telephone on her return from honeymoon and asking her how it was. I actually asked her if she was "any the worse for wear-and-tear?" and wondered why she didn't answer. Not the most tactful of remarks in the circumstances!

The stewardess arriving with the cart jolted me back into the present. Travelling Virgin had brought back some most unexpected memories!

Lonely Hearts
Barbara

I AM 43, FEMALE, CHEERFUL, solvent, quite sexy, rich in friendship and humor but lacking that one special man to share life's pleasures. Are you out there?

About 20 years ago it was an advertisement something like this, inserted in the Lonely Hearts columns of Time Out, which brought me 68 replies. I had advertised partly as a joke but partly as an acknowledgment to myself of the pain of living alone after 20 years of marriage. I had never anticipated so many replies, let alone thought through the process of dealing with them.

It was obvious that I could not fit meetings with 68 men into my life of work and family. I had to start a process of narrowing down. Out went all the married men wanting a bit on the side. Out went the schoolboys wanting experience with an older woman. And out went the few kinky oddballs suggesting weird and wonderful things we might do together. I made a first selection of six possibles who sounded interesting, were about the right age and lived within a convenient radius of my home. On advice from my women friends, who were following the experiment with fascinated interest, I established certain ground rules for myself: always meet in a public place; never give your address until you have met and decided it is safe; above all, don't expect too much. So, with these rules in mind, I embarked on a few weeks of hilarious activity.

Lonely Heart Number One

We arranged to meet outside the local tube station. He said he would sit in his car, which was a very special vintage something-or-other. I recognized the car by his description and we proceeded to sit in it for what felt like hours while he told me its history, year by year, detail by detail. He then suggested that we go for a drink but I declined, explaining that my four children were waiting for me at home. Lies of course—well, I have got four children but they were not waiting for me at home. End of LH No. 1.

Lonely Heart Number Two

We agreed to meet for a meal in an area where there are several good restaurants. When we met he suggested fish and chips, which he said he hadn't eaten for ages. Aha, I thought, he's afraid of being landed with the bill. All through the fish and chips he talked and talked—and talked. He was about fifty, lived at home with his parents, referred to as Mummy and Daddy, and did he have problems! I pulled out the trump card of my four kids and went home.

Lonely Heart Number Three

This one had got through the net. We met for a drink in Bloomsbury. He admitted to being happily married and looking for an exciting secret liaison. I bade him farewell.

Lonely Heart Number Four

Number Four was an expatriate American living in Richmond. We met on a lovely warm evening and sat outside a pub on the Green having a drink. I could not take in a word of our conversation because I was mesmerized by his head. Across his crown, in neat straight rows, grew little tufts of hair like young corn in a field. He must have just had a hair implant, the scalp underneath looked pink and inflamed. I could not take my eyes off it. Every time I tried to look away my eyes flickered back to his head. It was just no good—I didn't even need to bring in the four children. We agreed to part with thanks.

Lonely Heart Number Five

By now I was growing weary but I agreed to meet Number Five in a tea-shop, each of us carrying Time Out. I arrived slightly late and glanced in through the window. There he was, a shambling overweight man in a dirty raincoat, unshaven, greasy-haired. I am ashamed to say that I turned and ran, leaving him sitting there.

Lonely Heart Number Six

I broke the rules for Number Six. We had several telephone conversations and he sounded great, witty, sensitive and cultured. He was a successful painter, lived in a very posh area and was insistent that I came to dinner which would be prepared by his housekeeper—so I did. A flight of steps led up to his imposing front door. I rang the bell and waited nervously. As the door opened I pitched my eyes and smile at the height of an average man—then down, down, down to reach the level of his head. I am not very tall but I topped him by four or five inches. He wore flowing Arab robes which swung gracefully around his diminutive figure as he led the way into his beautiful sitting room. Everything was sumptuous, the food and wine delicious and the conversation easy and interesting.

After the meal he suggested that we watch Kenneth Clarke's "Civilization" and led me into another lovely room with a large television screen beyond which, at the touch of a switch, floodlit fountains played in the garden. There were no chairs in this room, just a huge bed piled with cushions. "Kick off your shoes and make yourself comfortable," he said. "Well," I thought to myself, "at least I'm bigger than he is if it comes to a struggle." And that's where it ended. The evening did not progress as he had clearly intended but he accepted my refusal with good grace, we parted friends, and I never heard from him again.

There were still many unanswered letters in my Lonely Hearts file but somehow the heart had gone out of it, leaving the loneliness. I felt diminished by the whole experience. There was something so sad and unfulfilled about all the men I met and yet, in the end, none of them asked to see me again. I was aware that I had given all of them clear messages of rejection but why weren't they begging for another chance to meet? Did they see me as sad and unfulfilled too? I found myself feeling even less attractive and lovable than before. I had no new answers to the problem of loneliness but at least now I knew that this was not the way forward for me. Maybe some people do find happiness by this route but my remaining letters went into the dustbin and, perhaps, amongst them was the nice, kind, sensitive, humorous man of my dreams. I'll never know. In those days it was still comparatively unusual to advertise through the Lonely Hearts columns but now every newspaper and magazine, from Saga to the Guardian, has column after column of cries from the hearts of lonely people of all ages and with all manner of needs. The old structures which held communities together do seem to be breaking down and, although I can now write about my experience in a lighthearted vein, it's really no laughing matter that so many of us have lonely hearts.

> **The important thing in acting is to be able to laugh and cry. If I have to cry, I think of my sex life. If I have to laugh, I think of my sex life.**
> *Glenda Jackson*

Shall I Never Feel Desirable Again?
Mary

At 70 there's not much to my sex life. And I don't spend much time regretting it either. It used to be important, now it isn't. And that's OK. It's a relief is celibacy—one of the joys of being old enough to admit it!

But I think about how sex has affected my life from time to time and I think it's important that women at this growing old disgracefully stage of our lives should be able to talk about it.

Whenever the question of sex comes up in a Growing Old Disgracefully group, there are some points we seem to agree on. One is how often women wish that men could be both physical and tender at the same time and not think immediately of going all the way. ("All the way!"—what an old-fashioned, useful phrase that is!) Another point, though agreed on much more tentatively, is that we ought not to be ashamed to admit that masturbation can be pleasurable at any age and need it be a last, lonely resort? Or why not, someone asks, try a vibrator?

By the time a group has come to this point there is probably nothing that cannot be shared!

One woman said, "I don't want to think that I shall never feel desirable again!"

Yes! We knew exactly what she meant.

Someone asked her, "Do you mean desirable just to a man or to a woman as well?"

There was a moment's silence. Then the answer.

"I hadn't thought of a woman—but I suppose, perhaps as I get older, it could be a woman."

It could be a woman! I've thought about that myself now and again…and in dreams and fantasies occasionally it is a woman who comes to me.

And there is a question we often leave unanswered. Aren't we all bisexual?

When I come to think about it, such a possibility makes sense. There were crushes and one brief, furtive sexual encounter I remember at my all-girls' school. But we were expected to grow out of it. Most of us did because there were such strong social pressures to be the one thing—unambiguously heterosexual and female.

We were so innocent and ignorant in those days! It was much more common for people to share beds. I remember that the two women who kept the village shop shared a double bed (I know because I saw it!) and some of our teachers shared flats together. Theirs was the generation of the "old maid" whose sweethearts, we were told, had been lost in the First World War. We thought nothing of it except to hope that our fate would be different.

So many of them were wonderful women and now I think of them quite differently. And I hope that their relationships, whatever their nature, were more fulfilling than we unknowing, unaware pupils ever guessed!

Celibacy

Anne

I love being on my own
I welcome the silence
I enjoy the empty space
Each hour is a blessing.

I love being with others
I welcome the communion
I enjoy the connection
Each day is a blessing.

Where does sex come in my life?
Is it important?

I love the feel of others
I welcome the caring touch
I enjoy each loving hug
Each kiss is a blessing.

And this is enough for me
In my new-found celibacy.

Dating
Shirley

One day recently when I was walking tall and feeling good about myself, I was stopped in the street by a young woman with a clip board. Me, a woman of 64, with grey hair, a carrier bag and a smile on my face.

She wanted to know if she could have two minutes of my time? Why not, said I.

"Are you married, single or divorced?" she asked.

"Divorced," I replied, with the happy rejoinder, "happily divorced."

"Which age bracket do you fit into?" Such a diplomatic way of asking a woman's age. But there was no need as I am proud of the fact that I am 64, and said so brazenly. "You sound happy about that," she commented with surprise.

"Why not?" I said. "It's a good age to be if you make it so." She looked at me, intrigued.

Then she told me she was representing a dating agency. Did I want to meet someone? I reminded her of my age but she said there were lots of men of that age out there looking for a woman companion.

I've been divorced 16 years now and without a relationship for eight. The last thing on my mind was to get a new partner, though I have often moped about being without one. Several of my friends had answered lonely-heart ads and had fun along the way.

Well, what did I have to lose, I thought. Certainly not my virginity. The clipboard woman took my phone number and said I would be contacted shortly with more information. The very next day, Debby from the agency rang. If I wanted, I could go and have a personal profile done tomorrow. They would show me a sample of the available men on their lists. It so happened that I was just about to go out and postponed a decision.

"Have a nice evening," said Debby.

They rang again next evening. This time it was Peter.

But I was going out again. "Are you already dating?" he asked.

"No, I just have a busy life." He got more curious and wanted to know more. I needed to leave and he got more and more interested, as I put him off again.

I resented the pressure but also wondered at my own motivation. Although I fancied an adventure, I wondered at my resistance, genuine though my postponement had been. Was it fear of meeting a stranger for the sole purpose of ultimate bedding? Was it the thought of "dating" that put me off, reminding me of having left the nervousness of such activities far behind me? Was I really in need of a man? Was not my lifestyle settled and joyous without the troughs and peaks of a sexual relationship?

I don't know the answers to these questions, but I suspect there is a bit of each in me as I found myself avoiding more calls from the agency. I'm surprised at myself having said so often, "Chance would be a fine thing". It is also contrary to my new spirit of adventure. But my gut feeling at present is to defer the date. After all, I'm too young for that sort of thing. Aren't I?

> **Old age isn't an illness, it is a timeless ascent.**
> **As power diminishes, we grow towards the light.**
> *May Sarton*

You've Lost So Much Weight!
Maxine

After spending many years learning to love my large body and feeling comfortable with being a "woman of substance", last year I became ill and lost about 40 pounds. It was not anything I set out to do, nor did I consider it an accomplishment. I would much rather have had my health back, and I definitely would not recommend such drastic means of weight loss.

It is difficult enough to come to grips with the changes my body is going through as a result of the aging process without having to deal with changing my self-image at the same time. I had to rethink how I moved through the world, how much space I did or did not take, how substantial I felt. Not that I am all that lean, but in comparison to how I was, it's a drastic change. Even small, inconsequential things became problematic, such as not knowing where to buy clothes, since for years I had been shopping in the large-size stores.

What bothered me most was the number of times people came up to me and exclaimed how great I looked, how much weight I had lost, and what was the secret of my success. Never mind that I felt terrible, that I could have been dying—the important thing was that I had lost weight. I know they were trying to be complimentary, but I felt as if they were saying I looked awful previously, and that somehow my worth was being measured by poundage.

I feel much better now, and have accepted my shape and size again. When people tell me I look great, I sometimes answer, "I thought I looked great all along, didn't you?" How's that for being a disgraceful old woman?

This Was Enough
Shirley

We drank side by side at the bar
He and I enjoying the whiskey's inner glow.
Greyhaired the pair. Mellow.
Chatting and laughing.
Casual.

Both part of a larger group
We'd met before, exchanged the odd phrase
But not really engaged.
Here and now
The ebb and flow of odd remarks
Deepened.

The clock ticked on and conversation blossomed
We warmed to each other's person.
Refills lubricating our voices
Coming from deep within us.
We enjoyed the time together.
Mutual attraction.
Others around us faded into haze.

The evening drew to a close
Feeling generous in heart to the other.
I glowed inwardly as a woman.
Publicly we parted, arms enveloping the other
Kissing affectionately. Two old bodies.
But this was enough.

Hysterectomy
Mary

Whenever the subject of hysterectomy comes up, I remember, often with some surprise, that I have had one myself. It was grim at the time and came as a shock. I was only 42—younger than my oldest daughter is now. It was following a positive cervical smear test. I was in hospital almost immediately.

What I remember most clearly from that time is not the worry and the dreadfulness of it all nor any of the crude jokes that were shared. What I do remember most clearly is all the laughter, lying in bed along both sides of the ward—all of us singing the songs and hymns we'd learned at school. We laughed and laughed and the stitches hurt and we still laughed.

The ward became a small closed world. We did not know the word sisterhood in those days—it was 1967.

When it came time to leave, it was hard to say goodbye. We had heard each other's stories, lived part of each other's lives, knew the worst and the best. It was quite a time till we lost touch with each other.

It's strange now to think of it. That was when I lost my womb. It should have been a great loss and a traumatic experience, but it wasn't.

Every year or so afterwards I had to have checkups. I did not like that at all. But I had gained some freedom. No more tampons or sanitary towels, no more dutch caps and no menopause to worry about. A very female kind of freedom!

> **Postmenopausal years can be the best of our lives.**
> *Mary Stott*

The Shapely Pad
Anne

Every time I see a TV advertisement for yet another shapely sanitary towel, I wonder how I managed for so long with the thick cotton-wool creation that I wore singly or in pairs through my early years of menstruation. Oh, the embarrassment of a red stain on my skirt or the greater dismay when the red blotch reached the cushion I had been sitting on in a neighbor's home. I remembered the stuffed paper bags carried prior to the onset and the reinforcements carried during the three- to four-day cycle in pocket, satchel, handbag or case.

I would have welcomed an initiation ritual, perhaps a bleeding on the moss in the forest or a ceremony to welcome me into womanhood. I received only commiseration for the inevitable and natural event called "the curse." Of course, I graduated to tampons which were so much easier to wear. The "old wives" said you should not use tampons while you were still a virgin, but my friends and I took no notice of that!

The new pad is wafer-thin, molded to fit the body rather like a hammock, with sticky edges to keep it in place. No need for the old sanitary-belt which I used to wear to hold the pad in position. Now there is a spray to obscure or camouflage the smell of blood which was so difficult to hide, the musty smell of drying, clotting blood. The blood that I used to pass every month for forty years, except on the two occasions it was used in the creation of a foetus. The blood I passed to show I am a woman.

There were no advertisements on TV then for pads or towels. The monthly period was always a taboo subject, a secret hardly discussed in the family and never mentioned to the men. Now young girls talk about PMT (premenstrual tension) and share the facts of their monthly blood-loss with their friends and family as a natural occurrence in their lives. Which it is.

Menopause replaces menstruation. Periods become irregular and eventually stop. No longer the ability to create a foetus (by natural means), no more need to use a tampon. I celebrated my menopause at my crone party. My ritual, a burning of the unused and unwanted protectors.

What a relief!

Linda

Sex After Sixty

Barbara

She had never thought of herself as a particularly sexy woman. She was more of the wifely sort, pear-shaped, comfortable, unglamorous. Her roles of mother and working woman seemed to define her as loving and giving but definitely not sexy. And as she reached her sixties she felt resigned to this definition. It was many years since her last sexual relationship and she was neither looking for nor anticipating another. She was content. Like many women, she felt a sense of relief when the aging process seemed to bring a lessening of sexual needs.

But then, one summer's day, as she walked across the park enjoying the warm sun on her back and humming to herself, she saw a familiar figure coming towards her. It was a friend whose company she had always enjoyed and whose friendship she had valued for many years. He had often half-jokingly suggested that they go away together and she had never taken the proposition seriously, treating it as friendly banter. But on this sunny day, with a spring in her step and a smile on her face she found herself thinking "Why not?" It occurred to her that she was now 61, that she really liked him and that it was more than likely that she would never have another opportunity for sex.

So when he told her that he had to make a trip to the south coast and smilingly asked if she would consider his suggestion again, as much to her own surprise as his she found herself agreeing to go away with him. And a few days later there she was, as coy as a virgin, arriving at a hotel in trepidation. Would it work after so many years? Would she feel too shy, too embarrassed to reveal her aging body? Would it be fun?

As they met in the hotel lounge, she saw that he was just as shy and anxious as she was. Women tend to forget that men too are aware of their bodies' aging. She realized that, in fact, it must be even more difficult for a man, for his anxieties could have such an adverse effect on his ability to proceed. She thought to herself, with a wry little smile, that it must make it harder but that is just what it doesn't do!

"Why are you smiling?" he asked, as they stood at the desk waiting to check in. She could not bring herself to tell him the real reason. She took his hand. "Because I'm happy."

In the end they were both so busy reassuring each other that they forget their own doubts and everything was fine—no, it was more than fine, it was pretty wonderful. She awoke with a feeling of joy and well-being, turning her head to find him smiling at her. Sleeping next to a man had become strange and unfamiliar to her after so long, she had almost forgotten the pleasure of just lying together, touching and talking.

Back in her own house she stood in front of her full-length mirror looking at her reflection with amazement. Who was this grey-haired old granny she could see? Whose was that old body, with its familiar folds and bulges? Her last thought before she went off to sleep that night was that sex ought to be available on the National Health Service. Because she felt lithe, alive, energetic and even disgraceful. And that was an unexpected feeling for an old-age pensioner.

> **Everything!**
> *Mae West, when asked what she wanted to be remembered for*

What Am I Missing?
Shirley

It's eight years since I felt a man's skin next to mine. Oh, how I hug my sons and touch men's arms of course. But anything lower? No tracing of form. No gentle stroking of limbs. No investigation of delicious creases. No unity by penetration. No awakening after the delicious sleep following intercourse with the loving body alongside. No sex.

Is it regret I feel, or is it relief? The sensuality is still there. I still feel sexual. I can still be aroused by the sight of a man's body though he belongs to someone else. I still have wet dreams when I awake moist with sexual secretions. My heart still races occasionally when aroused by erotic art, by romantic music, by the look in someone's eyes, by observing lovers.

I feel all these things but am not destroyed by the absence of physical love. I am resigned to so many things in old age. Reality reminds me of all the things I won't do now I'm approaching the final stage of my life. Like parachuting, ski-ing downhill, having more children, being a coloratura soprano. I'm not devastated by this knowledge. There are other things I can still achieve and explore—friendships, touching human hearts, writing, cycling (though a little slower), being a grandparent. Why then is the absence of sex so different when I still experience arousal? Is it the common reflection of society that a single woman without a man is forlorn, a failure, without femininity? Have I ingested this belief? Should I repress hopes of falling in love again, or enjoying a sexual encounter with or without love? Or should I make a decision to remain celibate from now on? Will that relieve the longing? A conscious choice is always better than resignation and defeat. So much more positive. But to be positive about what seems so negative. Is it really possible? Or even a good idea, to live without hope of this sort? Will I shrivel or will the absence of desire deaden me?

Maybe there is a compromise to be made. Maybe I should decide to be celibate for the present only. And be happy about it, appreciating all the other good things in life I can still enjoy. Recognize the unlikeliness of my being able to experience physical love and contact, but be open to the possibility. That way, my femininity can remain, my joy in life too, my appreciation of myself.

> **All one's life as a young woman one is on show, a focus of attention, people notice you. You set yourself up to be noticed and admired. And then, not expecting it, you become middle-aged and anonymous. No one notices you. You achieve a wonderful freedom. It is a positive thing. You can move about, unnoticed and invisible.**
> *Doris Lessing*

Sex and the Older Woman
Edith

I look up and see this dark-haired, attractive man staring down at me. His eyes seem to penetrate through to my inner core, right down to my waiting bosom. How fascinating, but how much longer can I go on with this fantasizing? I suppose I could make him a blue-eyed blond and the contact between us slow down, with all sorts of subtle overtures before we get to the stripping for the sex bit. What it all comes down to is wishful thinking. Where and how do older women, on their own, find sexual fulfillment? What if sensual sexuality was very much a part of a longtime relationship; the desire doesn't suddenly evaporate if for whatever reason the relationship comes to an end. Masturbation is a suggested substitute but it may not be every woman's solution, especially as it doesn't solve the companionship problem. If the opportunity does exist, why not sex after 75 or 80 or any age? Is it difficult to imagine old women in their aging bodies still wanting and enjoying sex?

I know it's hard, especially for young people, to visualize those situations. This is perhaps understandable since most of the media address their sex-angled work to a young audience which doesn't include old women. I was still unprepared for the responses of two of my granddaughters, now in their very late teens, when I asked them about the cutoff sexual age for women. One of them thought 50 years was probably the end for such goings on. The other gave us an extra ten years, until 60. At their age it must be difficult to look even ten years ahead for themselves but according to them I'm well past my time.

My fantasizing at the beginning of this piece was over the top, since casual sex, even if it were available, is not really the issue here. It's sex in the context of a relationship which brings with it companionship and the ability to share thoughts and feelings with someone else. Ideally, I suppose it's a whole package including the physical. Thinking about myself, the sensual aspect of sexuality became increasingly important in my aging relationship with my husband, eventually taking over completely. Feeling and touching was almost as satisfying as the act itself.

Age should in fact be no barrier to sexual enjoyment within a relationship. The key to it is opportunity. If it exists and is what you want, grab it!

> **Don't burden yourself with stupid, wrong notions about age and time. Don't tell yourself you've got to have made it by the time you're thirty, or that you're finished at forty, or a fossil at fifty. If you want a quiet life and to pass peacefully into gentle old age, do just that. And NEVER apologize for existing.**
> *Dorothy Rowe*

CHAPTER FOUR

Can I Break Old Patterns?

Dear Hens,

Since I retired last year my son and daughter-in-law seem to think that I am always available to baby-sit, night and day. At first I was happy to be needed, it gave my life some purpose. I love my grandchildren and enjoy being with them but I am beginning to feel that I need some life of my own. My son has invited me to go on holiday with them this summer but I can't help thinking how convenient it will be for them to take a baby-sitter with them. I feel that I would like to go on holiday with some friends of my own age. Do you think that I am being selfish? They are very loving and grateful and I don't want to hurt them.

Yours sincerely,

Rose

Dear Rose,

As women, most of us have grown up being taught to put everyone else's needs before our own. When the time comes that our responsibilities lessen, we have a hard time figuring out what would make our lives what we want them to be. We have played the role of caretaker, nurturer, soother of other people's feelings, peacekeepers. Now when it is our turn to pay attention to our own needs, we may find that we do not know what they are. But there's no time like the present to start breaking out of old patterns and looking at who we want to be.

It is always easier to stay in a prescribed role than it is to risk moving into a new identity. Even when you feel committed to change, there is much negotiation that needs to take place between you and those around you who have been accustomed to knowing you in your past roles. Partners or spouses may want you to stay the same so that they do not have to take stock of their own lives and make changes themselves. Children have a hard time visualizing you as other than "Mom." Friends of long standing may not comprehend why it is important for you to branch out into new connections, and may think you are abandoning them.

When you acknowledge this conflict, it makes your choices more conscious. You will recognize the difference between when you are being taken for granted or used, and when there is a genuine, compelling reason for doing what is asked of you. Shirley talks about this in her piece on "Their Needs or Mine?" and Barbara takes a look at her own way of grandparenting in contrast to her family models. Balance is hard to achieve, she says, but it is crucial if we are to find a way to grow into a disgraceful old age. So no, Rose, you are not being selfish in wanting to have a life of your own. You deserve to say, "It's my turn now", and in the process, you will be freeing your children to live their own lives.

Of course, not all women have children, and some who do are not close to them, either geographically or emotionally, but everyone experiences conflicting pulls at one time or another. It may be a coworker, a friend, or different activities calling for your time. Today, when people are living into their 80s and 90s, it might be an aging family member who wants your undivided attention, which could create resentments when you try to take care of your own needs as well.

It is important to recognize any negative feelings you may have about the people who are making demands on your time and energy. Decide how much you want to do and then do as much as you feel like doing but no more, so that resentments do not grow. Get others to help—call on family, friends, agencies, neighbors. Strive to create a balance between obligation and self-care, between the authentic needs of others and how much of those needs you should be expected to fill.

One of the first steps towards balance is learning to make your boundaries clear. You may feel strange when you first begin to respect your own need for time and space that is of your own choosing, when you let others know that you have limits, and you make those limits clear. Be patient with yourself, allowing for flexibility if the need arises. The only way you will be able to do this is to convince yourself that you deserve a life of your own, and that it is not being selfish to ask others to respect, whether they agree or not, that this is important to you.

When saying no, there is a tendency to make excuses that will soften the situation, as Edith's piece on declining an invitation shows. You do not have to justify your "yes" or "no"; just check in with yourself to see what you really want to do, then be clear in communicating your wishes. You might want to refer to Mary's assertiveness questionnaire in this chapter to help you get started.

Of course, it goes without saying that you must accord the same respect to other people's needs. If you are unwilling to be prevailed upon against your wishes, then you must accept that family and friends have lives of their own too, and not take it personally when one of your suggestions or invitations is rejected. Especially with our children, it is hard to let go of responsibility for them and respect their decisions. We may offer too much, as Shirley's conversation with her mother indicates. Ideally, you will have a relationship with your family members that shows that you have both a separate identity and a family identity, with each of equal importance.

Don't give up, Rose. If you need help in learning to say no, or in asserting yourself, or in bolstering your self-esteem, there are often free or low-cost courses through local authorities, schools, recreation centers and other venues. There you will find support and skills for making changes. A Growing Old Disgracefully Network group might be just the ticket. You are sure to find other women there who are supporting each other in their transitions. Good luck!

Disgracefully yours,

The Hen Co-op

Whose Needs—Theirs or Mine?
Shirley

Months ago my son and daughter-in-law planned a special outing, asking if I would be able to day- and night-sit their children. I desperately want to be close to my grandchildren though I don't see them often. This was an occasion to be with them which I welcomed as I'd have the whole day for that purpose.

Then came a date with my coauthors for a writing weekend together—which conflicted with the proposed day with the twins. A difficult decision had to be made. On the one hand I was fully committed to the writing but, on the other, I wanted to allow my children their day out. It wasn't a matter of duty but of wanting to be in both places at once. I had come a long way in my attitude towards growing old since I had long ago given an ultimatum to my son that he should make me a grandparent by the time I retired, thinking that this was the only likely preoccupation worthy of a woman pensioner. I have also changed in that I now realize what a selfish and unwise ultimatum that was without awareness of their needs, rather than mine.

I solved my dilemma on this occasion by putting the children first because of the earlier promise and they appreciated the decision in their favor, knowing that I was not one of those whose only existence depended on being available to them each and every time they needed help.

But it was an exception. When I retired five years ago, I realized the danger of not having useful things to do in the years ahead. I knew that I would need something to look forward to, other than endless days of TV, gossip, knitting and grandparenting, with which my mother filled her latter years. I went over the top in putting out feelers to needy organizations, saying in effect: Use me. I'm available. No wonder that I was inundated with requests for this and that. Victim Support, teaching English to refugees, community forums. local politics. I ended up gasping for breath, having to look constantly at my diary each day, wondering how I could fit everything in. It was harder work being retired than being fully employed! There was hardly time to see my friends and family, to have some fun.

As the years have progressed I have learned with an easier conscience to weed out, to say more frequently: No, I'm not able to help.

It is so easy to get sucked in, as I did throughout my life as a mother, dutiful daughter and wife. I still find it hard to put myself first as I still have this need to be needed. But I know that when I do—I find that those whom I need to need me—are in fact delighted that I have taken care of myself, that I am not the pathetic creature old women are so often seen to be, living solely through their children and thus a burden on them.

So my needs today are to live as vigorously as possible, and those I need to need me, need me that way. That seems very satisfactory all round!

Learning to Say "No"
Edith

Fending off with feeble excuses several persistent invitations from a couple I had met several months ago reminded me of an exercise that had been played out at a Women's Assertive Training Session that I had attended. Before it started, we were asked to assess ourselves on an imaginary line; one end was for the most assertive, the other for the least. I placed myself in the middle, playing safe, not being able to evaluate myself in that context. A role-playing exercise was then introduced as an example of assertive behavior. Two women immediately volunteered their service, while I was still in the throes of trying to decide whether I wanted to be involved in the exercise (not very assertive!). One of the women, Sandra, was inviting her neighbor, Ruth, to a Tupperware Party. The telephone conversation went something like this:

SANDRA: Hello, Ruth, I'm just telephoning to remind you that it's my Tupperware Party on Wednesday evening and I'm expecting you.

RUTH: Yes, of course I remember, but I'm really sorry I won't be able to make it as I have some friends arriving to stay that night, so it really isn't possible.

SANDRA: Oh, that's all right, just bring them along. I'm sure they will enjoy themselves. My parties are such fun and there is plenty to eat. So I CAN expect all of you.

RUTH: Have you forgotten, the boys have late night games on Wednesday and as I have to collect Tom, I really can't make it. Thanks anyhow for your offer.

SANDRA: Don't worry about Tom, we've made arrangements to pick up our John, so it's no trouble to collect both the boys at the same time.

Now I have cleared the way for you to come on Wednesday night.

RUTH: It's really kind of you, Sandra, but my sister is phoning me from New York that night and you can understand I must be at home to take the call.

SANDRA: Don't concern yourself about it, we can easily divert the call to our number, we do it all the time for Graham when he doesn't want to hang around his office when he's expecting a late call.

RUTH (caustically): You really are too kind, too good at arranging things, I still must beg off since Alice is going to camp on Thursday and I must get her clothes washed and ironed.

SANDRA: For goodness sake, don't give it a second thought. Bring the washing here. We can put it in my machine and since Deirdre is helping with the food she can do the ironing when there's nothing for her to do. There now, it's all settled and you and your friends can all come.

RUTH (quite forcefully): I can't possibly allow you to do all that for me. I will stay at home, look after my friends and get everything else done.

SANDRA: That is just ridiculous. You are my friend so why shouldn't I help you? Just come along with your friends and the washing. I'm sure all of you will have a great time.

RUTH (sarcastically): You are much too kind. The answer is still absolutely, irrevocably NO! I detest Tupperware Parties and don't wish to attend yours or anyone else's ever. (Hangs up)

SANDRA (very angry): I can't understand it. That's all the thanks you get when you try to help someone.

It was a tremendous performance. It was such a revealing exercise with both women being so assertive. I thought the contest would never end; then one of the women picked up the gauntlet and took it to an assertive conclusion. Vividly recalling that exercise made me realize that if I really want to say NO, whatever the situation, I must be prepared to say it and not fabricate excuses because at the time it seems the easier way.

Times Have Changed
Anne

I'm going to become a grandmother for the first time. It will be a new phase in my life, and it has started me thinking. Times have changed since I had grandparents or even since my parents were grandparents. I have very mixed feelings about the old patterns of regular contact and visits with their warm security and their claustrophobic entrapment. I broke the family traditions when I divorced and the family split up. I wanted to get out, be a person in my own right, and there seemed no other way to achieve this. It was the right decision at the time, but now I am to become a grandmother I want the family to come together again and I know it can't.

When I was a small child my parents took me and my brother (before my sister was born) every Sunday to my paternal grandparents, where I met my many aunts, uncles and cousins. My father was the youngest of six, and as his firstborn I was my grandfather's favorite. I used to sit on his knee, play with his fob-watch and comb his thinning white hair. We had "serious" conversations and I felt special. On my fifth birthday he wrote me a beautiful letter in his large sloping handwriting which started, "My dear darling granddaughter Anne," which I cherished until it was stolen with other papers in 1986.

When my own children were born, both sets of their grandparents expected us to visit every weekend so that they could see the children. On special occasions there were some divided loyalties and rivalry—whose turn was it to have us? In the last years of her life, family meant everything to my mother. Time spent with children and grandchildren were her most precious times. I have many interests and hobbies. Will I want to forego them in favor of family? Will I be given the chance or the choice? I know from the experiences of my family and friends that there will be no expectation of regular visits.

In past generations, all the strands of the immediate family lived near one another. Now we are widespread throughout the world. My grandchild will start his or her life living in the Far East. I hope to visit as frequently as I can, but that may not be more than twice a year. I hope the child will be brought to England from time to time. It will be difficult to form a special relationship, to look after the child and take it to interesting places, to live life vicariously through fresh and innocent eyes.

The mixed feelings of love and duty in earlier times have been replaced by an independence from family; being a parent or grandparent gives no special concessions. The nuclear family is a separate unit and makes decisions without recourse to the interests or views of the extended family. Love and respect have to be earned; they are not given as a right. I think that's how it should be, but I feel I have something to contribute to the new generation and I want to share some of my enthusiasms, some of my acquired wisdom.

For this, my first grandchild, I will probably be a voice on the other end of the telephone, a giver of cards and presents on birthdays and anniversaries. I won't be a valued elder, I won't have any part in molding this new life. I feel sad about it.

The Chain of History
Barbara

As I watch my grandchildren grow I have a powerful awareness of the continuity of life through women—each of us growing in the wombs of our mothers, our daughters growing inside us, their babies inside them in turn.

I was with my daughter when her daughter Annie was born. I was overwhelmed by the emotion, the joy of holding my little granddaughter just minutes after her stormy entry into the world. She was born cradling her cheek in her tiny hand, peaceful and full of character from the first moment.

I had found the perfect gift to give my daughter to celebrate Annie's birth, a set of lacquered eggs, each opening to reveal another smaller egg inside it. My mother, aged ninety-two, was delighted with her new great-granddaughter and we had a picture taken of the four generations of women. I often look at it and feel deeply moved by the thought that there, inside our little Annie, are her tiny ovaries and the eggs that may, if she chooses, produce the next link in the chain of history.

Not long ago Annie, now aged five, came to stay with me for a few days. My other three grandchildren live locally and came over to visit and play with her. Our days were full of child-oriented activities, swimming, going to the park, making houses under the table, cutting out, sticking, drawing, reading stories, dancing and generally having a lovely time.

My mind went back to the summer of 1936 when I was five. I was sent to stay with my father's parents for two weeks while my mother went on holiday. Both my grandparents spoke very little English, having come to England from the Ukraine as a young married couple. My father, their beloved younger son, had died when he was thirty-three and my mother had very little contact with her in-laws. I think that must have been the first time I was left there alone and I was lonely, confused, frightened and shy. I didn't know who these strange people were and they didn't understand what I was saying when I did speak to them.

I slept in a large high bed shared with my grandmother. Was grandfather banished or did they normally sleep in different rooms? The question did not occur to me. The bed was very different from my own small bed at home with its pink eiderdown on which I could imagine landscapes and adventures. This bed was covered by an enormous feather quilt, with a smooth white cover. The pillows were huge and soft too, I sank into them, was surrounded by them. Each night I would half awake as my grandmother came to bed, there would be a soft "oy veh" as she bent to take off her stockings, a sigh of relief as she removed her corsets—having of course donned her voluminous nightdress first. Then the bed would sink down on her side as she heaved herself into bed and peace would descend. At some time in the night I would feel the mattress bounce as she climbed out and reached for the large chamber pot which lived under the bed, then I'd hear a rushing torrent and back she came. In that bed I felt safe and warm but strange and lost too; I longed for my own familiar home. There was nothing in this house for a child to do, no other children to play with, no understanding of a child's needs. My grandparents were kind but their lives seemed unchanged by a child's presence.

Moving on a generation, what were my mother and mother-in-law like as grandmothers to my children? My mother believed that children should be polite, clean and well-behaved. Although she did love to see her grandchildren she was always critical of their behavior and never invited them to stay with her. As a result, visits to her flat were always duty visits, never anticipated with pleasure. My mother-in-law was very different, she loved her grandchildren unconditionally and was always willing to look after them or have them to stay with her, putting aside any other plans she might have made. She was a real granny to them and they all remember her with love. But we were the focus of her emotional life, she lived her life through us and the emotional pressure was extremely difficult to handle.

So neither of these grandmothers really got the balance right. Somehow we need to find a way to be free to live our own lives as we will and yet be there to establish and maintain real, loving relationships with our children and grandchildren. It is a balancing act, needing constant small adjustments to avoid the two extremes of selflessness and selfishness, neither of which are healthy. It is a joy to know that (for the moment anyway) my grandchildren come to visit because they want to and not as a duty. But it is also a joy to live my own separate life in which I am neither a mother nor a granny but just me.

Mary Ellen

My Grandparents
Anne

They hang on the wall
Opposite my bed,
My grandparents gaze
With benevolent eyes.
I feel their blessing
As I descend into sleep,
I know their love
As I rise in the morning.

Passe-partout frames one pair
Photographed in sepia
Formal, in a studio
At the turn of the century.
She like a queen
In her ice-pudding hat
Hair swept up
From her high-buttoned dress.
He, her consort,
With his twirly moustache,
Cravat at his throat,
With bright jewelled pin.

She died before my birth
Him I knew fleetingly.
They are part of my past,
They are part of my heritage.

What of the other pair?
Made of more solid stuff,
Image more modern
Creation of the thirties,
Respected citizens
Of the nineteen-thirties.
They spoiled me and praised me.
I sat on his sturdy knee
Handled his fob-watch
Combed his thin hair.

All four sets of eyes
Look out on my progress.
They are part of my past,
They are part of my heritage.

Mother Knows Best
Shirley

MY MOM: Don't forget to use the toilet before you go.

ME: I went half an hour ago.

M M: But you have a long journey ahead.

M: Mom. I'm 45 and I think I know when I need to go.

M M: Don't speak to me that way. I'm your mother.

M: I was just reminding you not to treat me like a child.

M M: I was only thinking of your good.

M: I can make decisions of that sort for myself by now.

M M: Remember when you had to stop on the motorway?

M: But that was for the children.

M M: You are too easy on them. And another thing I've been meaning to say. You let them get away with murder. The way they call you Shirley. Where's the respect?

M: I like being called Shirley. We're friends.

M M: But they answer you back. You should be stricter with them. They'll grow up and be cheeky. You'll regret it. And why don't they come and see me more often?

M: Perhaps they would come if you weren't so critical. You never leave them alone.

M M: But I only want it for their good. I know what's best. After all I brought you up and life wasn't so easy then. But I never expected a daughter of mine would go out to work and would leave her kids with someone else to bring them up. That's where they learn their bad behavior.

M: What bad behavior? Just because they answer back? That just means they're spirited and can stand up for themselves. And I prefer working to being stuck at home all the time.

M M: You should be at home. A mother's place is in the home. Oh, are you going now? Don't forget to use the loo.

M: Oh Mom, you haven't heard a word I said.

A Balancing Act
Mary

It would not be so difficult for women of my age to get the balancing act worked out if we hadn't been brought up to be *girls*—that is if we hadn't been brought up to be so *good*—always expected to be thoughtful for others, always so helpful! I don't think any of us ever learned to say a straight *no!* and get away with it!

Nowadays my granddaughter can say "No, I don't want to do that," to me much more easily than I can say it to her!

I don't always like it when she says it, of course, even if I defend her right to say it. And I'm sure I don't remember being able to say such a thing to my mother—ever!

I used to envy boys. They could be good *at* something (and be praised for it). We girls just had to be *good* and we didn't get the praise because it was how girls were expected to be. Trying to please everybody, needing everyone's approval, wanting everyone to like us—it's not surprising that it is still difficult for women of my age to say no to the people we love and whom we need very badly to love us in return, even at our age.

We can stand up for ourselves in shops and restaurants, we have no trouble taking our complaints to law officers, hospital authorities or any upstart bureaucracy you can think of; we can say no with aplomb when hawkers, Jehovah's Witnesses or salesmen come calling at the door. It's when personal relationships and emotional dependency come into it that saying no (and not feeling cut up and guilty about it afterwards) comes hardest.

Women of the next generation, our daughters and their daughters, know better. They practice *assertiveness!* Not that they always get it right, but they are more aware. Learning from them, I've found that practicing assertiveness can be useful at any age—and I've been both a trainer and a learner in Women's Assertiveness Training groups of all ages over the years.

There's a questionnaire on page 130, which I've often used in groups, that gives some idea of the sort of situations and issues that come up in Assertiveness Training. It would make a good starting point for Rose—especially as it has a score for Assertiveness at the end of it—though it is not meant to be taken too seriously.

Role-play is often a useful part of Assertiveness Training. It would provide an ideal opportunity for Rose to learn how best to deal with the kind of situation she describes in her letter. If you haven't done any role-play before, the idea of embarking on such a thing might be quite daunting. The first time is scary, the next is fun. Then it begins to get more serious.

The idea of role-play is to get some practice, something we allow for in many other walks of life, where it's safe to make mistakes, get some feedback about your own style and responses and some space to talk things over in confidence with other women.

Being assertive is not about being aggressive, nor does being assertive mean the person with the clout gets things all their own way. It is about clarifying relationships, learning to be more open with yourself and with others.

On the other hand I know from my own experience that an Assertiveness Training Group wouldn't necessarily solve all Rose's problems.

It's the training that we get in early life that is the hardest to unlearn. I want to be glad that my granddaughter can speak out her feelings more freely than the women of my generation were ever allowed to. And I think it's time we old women forgot about being so good and sweet and tried telling ourselves from time to time that it's all right to do what we want to do. It's not being selfish, it's all right to explain to our families, lovingly, assertively, how we feel about wanting time for holidays with our own friends, time for ourselves—as well as time for them.

And they will love us even more when we get back!

Seesaw
Shirley

Will he won't he give his seat up
As I straphang on the train?

I'm struck with this dilemma,
Shall I stand with pride or pain?

I want the seat with one sense
On the other pride resists.

Will he won't he see my grey hair
And give my knees a rest?

Or do I hope he'll see me youthful
Without need of such a gesture?

Life is full of contradictions,
While I long to sit with pleasure,

I'll be blowed if I'll admit to
Needing comfort and a doze.

Yet I'm tired and feeling weary
Will I won't I shift this pose?

And again, the man who sells the ticket
For the show, the train, the bus,

If he offers concession prices
Why is it that I fuss?

Who do I think I'm kidding?
I should really know too well

That my young disguise is thinning,
Old age has cast its spell.

But a bargain's still a bargain
More than welcome when one's old.

So the cheap price and the tube seat
I'll accept with grace, yet hold

To the will he won't he seesaw
Though I may dare even more

Cantankerous I may yet become
Demand my seat for sure.

What's yours is mine I'll state
So please, so please give way

I'll waste no time with vanity
Will you won't you make my day?

How Assertive Are You?
Mary

Here are some statements to consider so that you can find out just how assertive you are.

Read each of the following statements and decide whether you agree with them:

- If you strongly agree, **score 3**.
- If you agree only moderately, **score 2**.
- If you don't agree very much, **score 1**.
- If you don't agree at all, **score 0**.

1. Most people seem to be more confident and assertive than I am.

2. Sometimes I don't join in things I'd like to because I feel shy and inadequate.

3. When I know the food or service in a restaurant is poor quality, I find it difficult to make a complaint to the management. I always hope that someone else will do it.

4. I am always careful to avoid hurting other people's feelings even when I feel hurt myself.

5. I often find it difficult to be frank with my friends especially if I'm feeling critical of them.

6. I feel people often take me for granted and take advantage of me.

7. I don't enjoy making conversation with new acquaintances and strangers.

8. I often don't know how to give someone a compliment—even when I feel I want to.

Qieu

Can I Break Old Patterns?

9. I often avoid asking questions I'd like to ask for fear of sounding stupid.

10. I often feel I have no time for myself because people are making demands on me all the time.

11. When someone gives me a compliment, I'm embarrassed and I don't know what to say.

12. When someone asks me to help them I find it difficult to say "No."

13. I tend to bottle up my feelings rather than make a scene.

14. I am often afraid that people will find me boring.

15. I don't find it easy to express my opinions because I always think other people must know more than I do.

16. I often wish I could express more of the love I feel for my family and friends.

17. I often feel critical of myself even when I have done something worthwhile or important.

18. Sometimes I worry how people would react to me if I really asserted myself.

Now add up your scores. The lower your score the easier you find it to be assertive.

If your score is above **40** you need Assertiveness Training. If it's between **25** and **39** you could do with some practice. If it's between **15** and **24** you are probably as assertive as you need to be. If it's below **15** it could be you're a bit too sure of yourself. Think about it!

Hats, To Be or Not To Be
Edith

I stand in front of the mirror, looking at my dressed-up image; not the usual casual trousers and top today because I'm going to a wedding. Anne Woolf's son is to be married this afternoon and do you know what my big problem is? I cannot decide whether to wear a hat. If I decide the answer is Yes, should it be a small—or large-brimmed one?

A small dilemma by any standards, nothing compared to the traumas I experienced when trying to dress for my son's or daughter's major school events. They were the once-a-year afternoon occasions, almost always towards the end of the summer term. In those days, hats were considered an essential part of a woman's outfit and it was that item which most concerned my son. "Just wear something nice and plain," he would suggest, "and please, no fancy hats." As a young teenager, he couldn't cope with an outrageously garbed mother. My daughter was quite the opposite. The more unusual the clothes, with special emphasis on my hat, the greater was her approbation. My hat would be her means of identifying me to her classmates. My son would have liked me to be as unobtrusive as possible, to fade into the background, whereas my daughter had a different role marked out for me. She wished me to be visible, to stand out from the crowd and an outrageous hat could serve as the means. I did monitor my appearance, trying to keep a balance in my choice of clothes for those special events; allowing my children to call the tune during that period. It didn't last long but then neither did the fashion for hats.

Now that I have only myself to please, I have come to a momentous decision, I will wear a hat for today's important occasion, the wedding! It's one of my special ones—a large-brimmed, green straw with a matching band to my bright, multicolored dress.

CHAPTER FIVE

What Can I Do About Feeling Lonely?

Dear Hen Co-op,

I used to work as a secretary but now I've retired I miss the laughter we used to share in the office and I also miss the steady regular income. I live on my own and my family all live quite a distance away, so I don't see them very often. I've tried going to the Seniors' Club but I come home feeling even more lonely. What advice can you give me?

Best wishes,

Pamela

Dear Pamela,

Lonely—how that word resonates with the feelings of so many of us, old and young, rich and poor alike. We all have experienced loneliness at some time in our lives, as children, as adolescents, as young adults, or as we have grown old. We have been lonely on our own and lonely in the company of others, lonely in a difficult relationship or lonely at a noisy party. Why, then, does the loneliness of old age seem to have different, more frightening qualities?

As we age, we may not see as many possibilities. We may be dealing with ill health, reduced financial circumstances, deaths of loved friends and relatives, or perhaps we are living alone for the first time in our lives. As you point out, retirement can bring with it a loss of structure, self-esteem, status and camaraderie. All of these circumstances can create loneliness and a temptation to withdraw from the world.

Few people would choose loneliness. Solitude, on the other hand, can be comforting. It can be deep, contemplative, peaceful, a welcome haven which is essential for the creative mind. Sometimes the line between solitude and loneliness is fragile, though. You may be feeling fine about being alone, enjoying a good book or listening to the radio when, unexpectedly, the solitude becomes burdensome and tips over into loneliness. Whereas a day of solitude might have been welcomed when you were leading a busy life in the midst of many people, now too many of those days can become boring or depressing. And you may want different degrees of solitude at different times. As Anne says in her piece called "The Human Condition," wanting to be alone and wanting to share with other people can coexist.

You may never totally overcome feeling lonely. We all experience the feeling at times, as we describe in our pieces that follow. Coming into an empty house, a holiday, a piece of music, illness—so many things can trigger the feeling of being out there on a limb by yourself. At those times, remind yourself that there have been other times in your life when you suffered the pain of loneliness, and try to remember what strategies you used to survive those times. You had the strength to pull through then, and you still do.

As we talked about what we wanted to write for this chapter, we shared some painful memories and we were strengthened by recognizing the lessons we had learned. We know now that it is essential to have relationships that nourish our spirit, even help us to heal our bodies. We cherish the friendships that give us strength and connect us to other women with whom we share a common core of experience. Connectedness has always been the way women have negotiated their world, and it is doubly important as we age.

Many of our correspondents have written about loneliness, some like you asking what to do about it, others suggesting ways in which they have managed to overcome it. We must sound like a broken record by now, but in our own cases and in those of many who wrote to us, the difference seems to lie in what kind of a supportive group of friends one can connect with. So we say again and again, a circle of like-minded women makes all the difference in how lonely your days will feel.

Keep reaching out. Find people who share your interests. Be creative in searching out these potential friends. Until you try, you can never tell how many wonderful women are out there feeling as you do, looking for new acquaintances with whom to try out new activities. Are there any courses going on near you that might be of interest? It may be hard to go on your own, so is there someone you can call to join in with you so you feel more comfortable? Until you build up a new network of friends, you may have to be the one making most of the contacts. This may seem a lot of work, but the rewards are enormous and well worth the effort.

Living in a group situation may not be for everyone, but it is an option worth exploring as a way to lessen expenses and to create an extended family. As Jenny and June describe, their experience of living together has helped each of them cope with both finances and loneliness. With careful planning, any number of compatible people could pool their resources for rent and food, while still maintaining some privacy and autonomy.

You do not have to settle for loneliness all the time. Extend your hand and we bet someone will take it. And even at those times when you feel lonely, as inevitably will happen, you will be able to experience the loneliness without fear, knowing that you can reach out to one of your disgraceful sisters. You had courage to take the first step by writing to us. Build on that courage and try one disgraceful step at a time. We wish you much success.

Disgracefully yours,

The Hen Co-op

Alone/Lonely
Barbara

"Hello. I'm home!"

I close the front door and stand with my back against it in the silent hall. I do not speak the words aloud, they echo inside my head. Home.

There are times when my spirits are high and the empty house welcomes me in, peaceful, warm and bright. I feel at ease in my solitude, relish the silence. But today I stand in the hall and long for a welcoming voice—where've you been? what have you been doing? did you have a good time? Reluctantly I move, hang up my coat, check the answerphone for messages, put the kettle on. What an effort it is. I catch a glimpse of myself in the mirror. Who is this old woman I see? How did I get to this point in my life without noticing the passing of the years? I frown and she frowns back at me. I screw up my face in a grimace and find myself laughing—it's lucky there is no one to see this old woman making faces at herself in the mirror.

The kettle switches itself off with a click and as the tea brews I stand at the window looking out at my little garden. The spring bulbs are pushing through the cold wet earth, a magpie poses in silhouette on a distant roof, the winter sunshine is reflected by the raindrops on the leaves. I begin to feel better. I'll drink my tea and then phone a friend, make some plans. Oh, good, I haven't finished today's crossword and there are some delicious biscuits in the tin. Life's not so bad after all.

But there are days when it is much harder to lift myself out of the morass of loneliness and depression. Some of the hardest times come if I am feeling ill and long for some tender loving care to get me through the day. Not long ago, after a few days of coping with the effects of a cold and its accompanying depression, I met some old friends, a married couple of about my own age. I am sure that their marriage is not perfect, in fact I know that they have had some bad patches but as they left to drive home together and I drove home alone I was swept by such strong and passionate feelings of loneliness that I had to stop the car until I could deal with the physical effects. The pain felt so acute that I could not breathe. But the moment passed, I started the car and drove slowly home.

How can we find the strength to deal with the loneliness which stems from the lack of a significant other for whom you come first and who comes first for you? Perhaps maturity brings the recognition that ultimately we are all alone and must find the strength to survive within ourselves. Perhaps when I grow up I will stop being envious of others. Envy is such a waste of energy. It is very possible that the wife I envied is envying my freedom. I do, after all, make an effort to appear cheerful, busy and fulfilled and usually that effort itself does make me feel better after a while. And then friends call or I call them and we meet and share our news and feelings and affection. And then the sun comes out from behind the clouds.

The Human Condition
Anne

I am walking through the fallen autumn leaves, scrunching their dryness under my feet. I am looking for fallen chestnuts, feeling their smooth silky sheen. I am alone in the autumn of my life and able to experience these pleasures without interference, without distraction. Another time I am with a friend, collecting autumn leaves newly fallen, still full of sap and color. We make a sculpture joining the leaves together with small twigs, like assembling pieces of material with pins. We add feathers, berries, wildflowers until we have built up a collage of nature. We go to the edge of a pond and lay our offering on the water and watch it glide slowly away on the ripples. Together we have created something of beauty with its temporary, ephemeral quality.

These are two facets of life which give me pleasure. I love to be alone and I love to share with other people. I like to share time with someone quiet and reflective. I like to share time with someone with energy and enthusiasm. How can one person meet all the needs of another? How can life be organized with time alone and time with others to provide the right balance?

One of the things I now know about myself is that I am threatened by intimacy. I need people, but I need them for limited periods of time. When I feel as though they intrude upon my much-protected privacy I back off. This is difficult to accept because I still want loving relationships. I want the giving and receiving, but with an ambivalence which leaves me high and dry on an island of my own making.

When I am feeling low and depressed I long for someone to look after me, to allow me to regress to a helpless baby. When I am feeling good with myself I want to give to others, I want to be generous with myself as others are to me.

In the end, I know that however many people we surround our-selves with, we are alone. Alone with our own thoughts and feelings. We can express these to others, be heard and understood, be loved and cherished, but we are still alone. That is the human condition.

Eve and Martha

A Correspondence
Edith

10 April 1993

Dear Ladies,

I happened to be home from work one morning and saw your group on a TV program. It was connected with a book you had written. I was very impressed with the things you said. It made me wonder what my mother would have been like had she the opportunity to meet up with such a lively lot of ladies. My mother is just the opposite. She is 62 years old and hasn't had a particularly easy life. She married my Dad when she was just 19. Money was always tight, the children always came first and then there was my Dad. He was a very good person, but not someone you would call talkative or particularly cheerful. After a long week's work in the factory, all he wanted to do was sit in a comfortable chair and watch TV. They never had what I would call real holidays. My Dad died a few years ago and by that time, we children had left home. My brother went to Australia, he doesn't keep in touch, and me in London. My mother is a very sad and lonely woman although she won't admit it. Do you think you could put her in touch with some women who live in her neighborhood? She is Mrs Jane Halstead and her address is 27 Ravenscroft Road, Harrogate. I do hope you can help her.

Yours sincerely,

Rita Halstead

Dear Mom,   15 April 1993

    Sorry I haven't been to see you recently but
I have been so busy at work that when the weekend finally arrives, I'm too tired to do anything and seem to just rest, then it's back to
work on Monday morning. It was certainly much
easier when we could at least speak to one another but since you decided to disconnect the
telephone because nobody except me called you,
it's back to letter writing. You may not realize
it but I do think about you a lot. In fact I
wrote a letter asking for information about a
group that could be so good for you. I saw a
program on television one morning when I was
home from work with that really heavy cold. It
caught my attention. It was about a group of
women who had written a book called *Growing Old
Disgracefully*. They were in their sixties and
seventies. They spoke about themselves and how
they had met, but what impressed me was what
they said about old people and how they could
still enjoy themselves and really enjoy life.
They are trying to set up groups of older women
all over the country. I was sure this would
interest you. It might give you the opportunity
to meet other women. It could be fun. I sent
them your name and address, so I hope you will
receive something soon. Hope it's still all
right for the weekend of 8th May. I'm really
looking forward to it. We'll have a good gossip
and I'll tell you the latest about my job and my
minuscule social life.

Love,

    Rita

Dear Rita,   18th April

I read your letter several times as I just wouldn't believe my own eyes. Who gave you permission to write off on my behalf as well as giving my name and address to some weird organization you saw on T.V. I do think you might have told me about it first before going off and doing something as ridiculous as that. I don't need new friends or anybody else for that matter. I'm quite happy on my own with nobody to please except myself. As for the telephone since it wasn't being used except to speak with you, there didn't seem much point in spending all that money.

Incidentally I have never received anything from an organization so probably nothing will come of it or if I do hear from them, it will be to request money for membership to something I neither want nor need. In the future don't do anything for me without consulting me first as well as letting me see beforehand what you have written. In fact now that I think of it I insist on seeing what you wrote about me to absolute strangers. You can bring it along with you when you come on the 8th.
Love from
    Your mother

Dear Mom,   23 April 1993

    I was really upset when I received your letter telling me off for trying to help you. I was only doing it for your own good and my peace of mind. Perhaps I do feel a bit guilty about not

seeing you more often, but more important I really would like to think of you enjoying yourself, laughing and doing things with other women.
I know Dad kept you away from all that when he
was alive, but he's gone now so you ought to
catch up on all the things you missed all those
years. Be a little disgraceful, that's what those
women were saying on that TV program and they
didn't mean anything scandalous, just doing your
own thing and having fun too.

I'm really sorry if I have made you unhappy.
I will see if I can find the letter I wrote to
the publishers of that book although I'm not sure
you will agree with everything I wrote. Hope the
weather up north has been better than London.
It's been wet and windy here. Let me know if
there is anything I can bring when I come on the
8th.

Love R.

Dear Rita,   28th April

I have a good mind to tell you not to come on the 8th. What do
you mean when you say that you wrote things about me that I
might not like. I think it's time you showed me that letter so be
sure you bring it with you when you come for the weekend.

Your mother.

Dearest Mom,   11 May 1993

    Thanks for a lovely weekend. I think in spite of what you were feeling about me before I arrived, things worked out well. I know for the first time ever, we really talked. I also realize it was wrong of me to have written to those people before asking you but it was my wrongdoing that helped us get much closer together. We were both angry, you especially, I've never seen you like that before. You told me things about your life that I never knew. You actually admitted to your sadness and loneliness, and I could tell you about my unhappiness too. We both faced up to truths about ourselves. As if that wasn't enough for one weekend, that reply arrived giving you information about a group of women in your area. Even you had to admit it might make it possible for you to meet new people and get out more.

    I am truly sorry I did something on your behalf without consulting you. You were right and I was wrong. Let me know if any of the women get in touch with you. It probably would have been easier if you still had your phone.

Your loving daughter
    Rita

Dear Rita,   15th May

    I'm glad you enjoyed your weekend. I did too and I'm sorry I carried on the way I did at first but as you say it did help us to talk in a way we never had before and brought us closer together. We do understand each others feelings better. Incidentally I had a letter from one woman on that list, inviting me to a gathering at their house next week and although I'm a bit scared I intend to go. I've no idea what it will be like but as we agreed if I don't respond, I will never change my life. Our heart to heart made you realize that you had problems in your life which had to be looked at too. Why did we wait so long for this to happen? So next week I'm off to this unknown adventure. I'll let you know what happens.

Your loving Mom.

Dear Mom,   18th May

Do let me know how that meeting went and whether you found the women friendly. What did you talk about? How many women were there? I'm really anxious to know. There's no news about me but I will write a longer letter after I have heard from you.

Love
Rita

Dear Rita,   22nd May

I knew you would want to know about everything as soon as possible, so here I am. I haven't enjoyed myself in this way in a long time. The women were so welcoming. We were nine including me. At first, they each told me very briefly something about themselves which made it easier for me when it was my turn to speak about myself. We did some writing about childhood memories. Mine was terrible but it was the first time I ever tried anything like that so maybe I'll practice a bit at home. It was interesting to hear what the others had written and they didn't think mine was so bad. There was also a discussion about future plans which included a possible trip to the theater in London, if they can get the tickets. Someone said the play had had very good reviews. Then we played a game, telling a story two words at a time. I couldn't get the hang of it at first, but when I did, it was really funny. At one point I just could not stop laughing.

I was wondering if they do get these theatre tickets, maybe we could manage to meet. I can't believe that I never visited you in all the years you've been living in London. Incidentally, I'm seriously thinking of having the phone re-connected. It might be useful with all this going on. I just hope it won't cost too much. Of course it does mean a bit of skimping and maybe going into my savings, but what am I saving for, if not to enjoy myself occasionally. I'll let you know if and when the telephone is connected.

Thanks again for disobeying your loving Mother.

The Loneliest Time of My Life
Barbara

I started my married life in two unfurnished rooms in a large shared house in a London suburb. The house hummed with life, children, babies, neighbors, friends, the coffee-pot always on the go, conversation, laughter. It was there that our first son Steve was born and the presence of older, more experienced moms was enormously comforting and supportive since I was just twenty-two and had had no experience with babies. But then, when Steve was ten months old, Julian changed his job and we moved from this warm loving community to Darley Abbey, a little village on the outskirts of Derby. We managed to scrape together enough money to buy our first house—it cost $2500 and the down payment was $200. The year was 1954.

The house was in a lovely position, with a large back garden running down to the river Derwent and an open prospect at the front. We had very few possessions, no car, no telephone, no carpets, no washing machine; there was, of course, no central heating and we didn't even have an indoor toilet. We moved in February, in a snowstorm, travelling from London to Derby in the back of the removal van. Then, the very next morning, Julian went off to work and Steve and I were left alone in this strange, cold, silent house. Poor little Steve was bereft—why was it so quiet, where had all his little playmates gone? He would not let me out of his sight, certainly not for long enough to put my boots on and wade through the snow to the outside toilet! Nor could I take him out there with me. In desperation I was reduced to using a bucket which I rushed out to empty as soon as he had a nap. The only means of heating the water was a back-boiler in the sitting room but every effort to light it resulted in clouds of smoke billowing into the room. I sat on the bare boards hugging Steve and cried. I had never felt so lonely and miserable.

The days stretched ahead interminably. I worked hard to run the house and manage our meagre finances. I learned to make clothes, bake cakes, bread and biscuits, stretch the meat ration (meat was the last item to be rationed after the war, 1954 being probably the year rationing ended). I was desperately lonely and counted the hours until Julian came home from work each day. It seemed so hard to make friends in the village, our neighbors believed in keeping to themselves and friendly overtures were rebuffed. We were so different and I can see now that our easy-going ways must have been offensive to them. I remember one glorious summer's day when I had put a tub of water in the side yard for Steve and he was busily painting the shed, the warm sun rapidly drying his handiwork. As I stood reveling in the beauty of his little naked body in the sunlight there was an angry knocking at the front door. Did I realize that he was out there with nothing on? It was disgusting and would I please do something about it immediately? As a result of this incident our neighbors erected a six-foot wall between our two houses and were never again offended by the sight of a small naked child. Oh how I longed for a friendly human voice.

As the days, weeks and months went by life did become slightly less desperate. Bit by bit we improved our material surroundings; we put in an indoor lavatory, installed a hot water heater and bought some cheap felt carpeting to cover the boards. Without a vacuum cleaner or even a carpet sweeper I had to use a dustpan to get up the crumbs and that was a chore I saved to coincide with listening to Mrs. Dale's Diary on the wireless (as we called it then), a daily lifesaver. In fact I even listened to the repeats, feeling comforted by the kind friendly voices. To this day the action of kneeling on a carpet to brush up crumbs brings those voices to my mind.

Those two years were the hardest and loneliest I can remember, yet our marriage was happy, we were dealing with adversity together and Julian did his best to improve our lives. The problem was that, because of the circumstances, I could not develop any independent life of my own. I began to realize that this was not enough, that I had to find my own interests and my own friendships, above all friendships with other women, and not live my life through my husband and children.

Celebration
Mary

I'm glad you've come she says
My friend—waiting—ready to hear
What I have to say.
The little world we have to talk about
Has shrunk because
Beyond this present is the unspeakable
Gaunt and vast and close to death.

And so we smile.
I tell her how yesterday
Quite dark at night
Two visitors came knocking at my door
Daughter and grand daughter
Laughing because I'd been taken by surprise.

And so we smile.
And now she tells me
"I met someone today
By chance—someone I haven't seen for years—
Our age and into tap, tap dancing, just for fun,
Something I've longed to do myself for years."

So we smile.
Say we could celebrate this little world
Precious and shrunk and circumscribed.
It will pass we say. And so it will.
And yet
Beyond this present the unspeakable—
Gaunt and vast and close to death—
Will it pass we say.
Will it pass?

Plain Gold Wedding Ring
Shirley

Plain gold wedding ring
My father wore for married years.
A solitary adornment
Signifying ties, loyalty,
Responsibility to family.

He died too soon
Ambitions unfulfilled.
And while he drew last breath
I held his hand
And felt this symbol on his finger.

My mother lived on fourteen years
That ring upon her finger
Withdrawn from his
While body chilled
Which I in turn took from her.

I did not wear it
Though treasure it remained.
I'd gaze and feel its meaning
Linking me with him
I loved so dearly.

One day a burglar came
And snatched this sentiment, this memory
Together with more mundane things
All replaceable in time.
But not that plain gold ring.

Healing Ceremony
Maxine

Last year, after a perfectly delightful, exciting spring and summer, I became ill. Exhaustive and exhausting tests and examinations revealed that my liver was being attacked by the Hepatitis C virus. According to medical "experts," there was really nothing to be done for it, a depressing thought indeed. I was feeling so bad that I was at the point of not wanting to live at all, if that was how I would have to be for the rest of my life.

I tried to carry on with as many of my normal activities as I could, but my days began to consist of perhaps a few hours of work and the rest of the time in bed. I was in constant pain. I could not eat, had trouble with the smallest tasks, and my mental state declined to the point that I had trouble holding on to a thought long enough to finish a sentence. Simple ideas became muddled and complicated. In short, I was a wreck.

When I was at my lowest point a friend came to visit, took one look at me, and said, "This cannot go on." She called on another friend for help, and they mobilized others. A collection was taken up, and they arranged for a delivery of meals to my door every week for several months. My laundry and shopping were done for me, offers of transportation and other services came pouring in.

In the meantime I had consulted a medical doctor who specializes in natural healing methods, primarily through diet and nutrition. He put me on a very strict food regimen and reassured me that I would get better. My spirits began to rise immediately. I was willing to do almost anything to be able to function again, so a few dietary restrictions seemed little enough sacrifice.

But to complicate matters, one of the diagnostic scans revealed a growth on an ovary, and I was being advised to have surgery. I was not at all sure that my liver was going to like the anaesthetic any better than I was, and I felt as if an operation would stir up the hepatitis even more. One doctor told me definitely to have the surgery because ovarian growths are not usual in postmenopausal women, and cancer was a possibility. Another was advising against the surgery. I was having a hard time trying to make the decision. It was then that I came up with the idea of asking some of my friends to hold a healing ceremony for me.

I have never been a person to put much faith in the power of spirituality, so it seemed rather out of character for me to be requesting such an event. I told my friends that because they had been showing so much love and caring I knew in an abstract way that help was out there, but I wanted to make it more concrete. I wanted to make it part of my being, to take their love as healing energy into my body.

So on a chosen Saturday morning, nine women friends gathered around me. A small prayer rug had been set up, on which they had arranged personal, meaningful objects. Each in turn gave a healing bless-ing in her own tradition: there were Hebrew prayers, Buddhist chants, African praying in tongues, Native American ritual, secular wellwishes, goddess blessings, affirmations of all kinds. I lay on the floor with my head on the prayer rug while all these strong, beautiful, loving women put their hands on me, and for the first time in my life I felt the power and validity of the laying on of hands. My body was infused with heat, I trembled involuntarily. Tears flowed all round, cleansing fear and de-pression out of my body.

I had the surgery (the tumor was benign) and recovered quickly. I never even took a painkiller and was back at work in two weeks. Who knows what difference, if any, the healing ritual made in my physical healing process? Without a doubt it made a great deal of difference to my emotional state, and I am convinced that one's state of mind greatly influences physical well-being and vice versa.

Every illness can be a time for reflection, for learning something about ourselves. When I asked a friend of mine what her breast cancer and subsequent mastectomy had taught her, she replied, "I learned that I am loved". I think that sums up what I learned also. And a very im-portant revelation was that I could *ask* for what I needed without wait-ing for others to offer. What a disgraceful idea!

My friends thanked me for the privilege of being part of this brilliant exchange of energy, for allowing them to show their appreciation. So it was a double blessing—I got what I needed and those I asked felt good about being able to help. Isn't that what this life should be?

To My Mother
Mary

Today when I saw you standing there
at the door, to say goodbye
Knowing you're going to be alone
When I have gone (and glad to go)
Did your eyes fill with tears
But behind the door, that I should not see?
Did your face stare back into the empty house
Listening for my voice
Still to be where we started
When it was all to be planned
and looked forward to?

Oh I know but I dare not tell you
That I know what the door's shutting means
(the tears and the listening the same)
I am the mother and mine the daughter who goes.
It is I and not you at the door to say goodbye
Knowing I'm going to be alone
When she has gone
And can she be—as I am—
Glad to go?

Another New Year's Eve
Edith

January 1st

Woke this morning with the most dreadful headache, my head was really pounding. At first couldn't think why. Then I remembered; I had drunk most of the champagne the previous evening. It was awful stuff, but then I was feeling pretty awful myself. I can't think why I economized suddenly and bought that bottle instead of a decent vintage. If I had I might not be feeling so dreadful now.

Of course, last night was New Year's Eve. Turned into another depressing anniversary. Why should I expect it to be different from other evenings? I suppose I attach too much importance to specific dates, associating them with events that belong to other times. I think it's just wishful thinking; the desire to replicate happier occasions. This year we didn't even attempt a proper celebration; having decided not to stay in Devon with our family and their friends, we returned a few days before the 31st. I did vaguely consider telephoning around to friends who might not have had any plans for that evening, but quickly rejected it as I couldn't summon the energy or the enthusiasm to get it together. So it was agreed that C and I would see the New Year in on our own; create our own fun and have the champagne all to ourselves. The evening was a minor disaster. We ate the super meal I had prepared and if I do say so myself, it was good! I worked overtime to maintain a semblance of merriment, but I just couldn't keep it going on my own. C wasn't up to even a modest contribution. We kissed and hugged at midnight. Each of our kids telephoned soon after to wish a H.N.Y. Wanted to know of course how things were. I wasn't about to share my misery with them at that point. They know but we'll talk about it more another time. It was after their calls that I drank most of the champagne, overwhelmed by a sense of loneliness. C had taken himself off to bed and I cleared the remains of our non-celebration, my wretchedness increasing with each dish and glass I washed. It was probably somewhere around 3a.m. when I finally joined him in bed.

Enough of last night. I'll drink some more water, get some lunch for C and perhaps go for a walk on the Heath.

January 2nd

Feel much, much better, My head has cleared and the gallons of water I drank must have done the trick. This clarity has reinforced some vague thinking that began to surface yesterday. I suppose I could call them New Year's resolutions. I'll try getting them down and see if that helps. 1. Because of C's illness, I'll try to accept his inability to participate on a level satisfying to me. 2. Try to be more understanding of his difficulties and recognize the realities of our current life. If at all possible I'll try to initiate activities on a level satisfying to me and no guilt feelings about that! 3. No more wishful thinking! 4. Try to make regular diary entries, don't put it off for whatever reason.

Carry On Dancing

Anne

(with apologies to Hilaire Belloc)

Do you remember a dance
My Hen-Friends?
Do you remember a dance?
And the flowing and the glowing
The puffing and the blowing
And the knees that freeze from arthritic jointing
Lifting, drifting, pointing and anointing.
Moving in a circle,
Lined-up in a column
Music lilting, toes a-twinkle,
Faces radiant despite the wrinkles.
And the Hip! Hop! Hap!
Of the clap
Of the hands to the twirl and the swirl
Of old girls gone chancing
Glancing,
Dancing,
Backing and advancing.
Standing on the down-beat
Moving on the up-beat
Swaying like trees in a gentle breeze
Slower and faster with movements that please.
Flashing, dashing, sometimes even crashing,
Raising, phasing, wondrous and amazing
Forevermore,
My Hen-Friends,
Forevermore.

Going Solo
Shirley

Approaching 50 I was alone, recently divorced, with both sons capable of looking after themselves, and I needed a holiday. I was into defying the fates with a new job, new miniaturized home, degree studies and beginning to put the acrimony of separation behind me for a more positive future.

Having previously always gone along with my husband's plans for holidays, following behind him as a dutiful wife, allowing him to do the talking, the negotiation, I decided to celebrate my 50th birthday with a deliberately solitary, coast-to-coast Greyhound bus ride across the United States.

I wanted to start from Boston and end up in California, then on to Vancouver to visit my family. All I booked were my outward and return journeys and a coast-to-coast Greyhound ticket. I knew no one in the U.S. A friend put me in touch with a contact in Boston who would put me up for the first night. That was a happy break as she knew others across the States and proceeded generously to phone them all to ask them to welcome me en route.

In all the four weeks I was away I only stayed in hotels three nights. Sleeping overnight on the coach a couple of times provided another economical way of moving on. For all the rest, hospitality was showered on me by complete strangers.

I had planned a route but it was flexible enough to suit my own whims and offers of a free bed. I found that talking to strangers was easy and enjoyable—quite different from the experience of observations and the oohs and aahs on seeing interesting landscapes shared with a familiar travelling companion. The more intimate feelings were noted in my personal travel notebook.

Despite my adventures and casual meetings along the way it was a solitary experience, but I wasn't lonely. There was too much to enjoy both in the travelling and the pleasure of my own company. It was a wholly surprising and enjoyable awakening.

Since then I have spent many holidays alone or with a group previously unknown. Many of my friends were teachers who could only take time off during expensive vacation periods. I was not limited to that and yet I was fortunate to have about five weeks annual leave from my job. I wanted to see as much of the world as my earnings would allow and not be limited to fixed packages only. No Shirley Valentine holiday romances came my way but good friendships did.

Sharing bedrooms with strangers is one of the worst aspects of holidays when you can't afford the single supplement—an iniquitous charge on the solo traveller. One time I could not tolerate the room sharer whom I had been allocated by the tour operator. She read far later into the night than I. She managed to trip over every obstruction she had casually dropped the night before—like bags, shoes—on her frequent trips to the loo during the night. I avoided her like the plague during the day and caught up on my sleep on my return home, but I couldn't have afforded that trip to then-Czechoslovakia had I taken a single room. The only time sleeping arrangements really worked was when I shared with my Hen Co-op mate Mary. Both of us snore but Mary's deafness is far worse than mine so I didn't disturb her and my depth of sleep was greater than hers. We both slept well!

One of the other things I find difficult about solitary holidaying is mealtimes. The restaurant may boast panoramic views but these are not for the solitary diner, doubling the irony of their high-cost room supplements. The single woman gets the corner table, darkened by the constantly swinging doors to the kitchen. It's as if there is shame heaped on her. She shouldn't be on her own, shouldn't be seen—an embarrassment to all. She doesn't portray the happy holiday image of the exaggerated brochures. I don't like "being put" with other diners I don't know. When I've chosen a solo holiday I don't want to be forced to make polite conversation all the time. If friendships develop naturally, well and good, but I often prefer eating alone, even if I have to keep my nose in a book to avoid the glances of the couples whose women see me as a potential threat. If only they knew how well I cope without a man.

If I'd waited for others to be available for my various treks I might never have got to where I went—and denied myself a lot of fun. Holidays alone are certainly different and they require some courage. But once done and you've managed to make yourself understood by actions and grimaces in a country whose language you don't speak, it's never as difficult again. Once I drew pictures in the sand to make myself understood. Another time I acted as if in charades. Sometimes I made myself understood, at other times I caused much amusement for others and frustration for me. But it's all part of the adventure.

Often it's cheaper to travel off-season to exotic places than attend a study course at home. I've tried those and they're often wonderful but somehow I always feel old there. But the experience of travelling alone, as an increasingly old woman, in contrast, gives me a spark of youthfulness and derring-do in my soul that gives my life relish.

Life is too short and the world is too wide to just be satisfied by the TV travel programs. Pardon me while I skim through next year's brochures. I feel an adventure coming on.

> **Life is finite. We should make the most of it.**
> *Dorothy Rowe*

Loneliness

Barbara

(with apologies to Wordsworth!)

I wandered lonely as a cloud—
But loneliness is such a bore
It hangs upon you like a shroud
A heaviness you can't ignore.
Beside the lake, beneath the trees
It nearly brings you to your knees!
Too high a hope of happiness
Can disappoint and lead to pain,
But solitude, not loneliness,
Is something we could all attain,
For, in the end, we're all alone
Despite the friendships we have known.
And often as in bed I lie,
Alone and in a pensive mood,
I like to think that, when I die,
I'll look back feeling life was good—
And then my heart with pleasure fills
And dances with the daffodils.

Angeline

What Can I Do About Feeling Lonely?
163

A Story: Woman Alone
Mary

While it was still light it felt bearable.

Now that it was beginning to get dark Peggy wondered—were people looking at her?

But she stayed where she was, sitting alone on the bench on the Embankment. Glinting between the branches above her head, all at once, an evening star. It made her gasp, so beautiful it was—held out to her by some unseen hand like a jewel from the darkening sky.

She noticed the tree above was an almond, coming into early blossom. Peggy shut her eyes and instead of the stark half-opened buds above her she filled her mind with branches laden with mounds of pink blossom as they would be later—the sound of the cuckoo calling—the sudden unforgettable sight and smell of bluebells.

All the promise of the spring and summer to come! Could this be happiness in Spring—a woman alone—newly separated and 57?

A young couple joined her on the seat, she moved up, feeling self-conscious—safer that way though—now it was dark—with the couple sitting next to her. She could go home to the empty room… "On such a night as this…On such a night…" The couple sitting next to her were silent—sitting apart. It was getting cold. The London traffic roared along the Embankment behind her. Opposite, across the river, the lights grew, now separate, now together.

She stood up to go.

"Good night," the woman on the bench said, then added, unexpectedly, "Good luck!"

A prostitute—did they think she was a prostitute?

She stood for a moment in front of them, wary, curious.

"It's not luck I need!" she said—"It's a good job!"

"Not a husband!" the woman said.

"No—not a husband—just a job!" They laughed—warm, friendly; but the man said nothing.

It was all right. As she walked away she felt elated, glad of the little encounter—not a husband, a job—that's what she had said. It was all right and she could say so. They hadn't taken her for a prostitute—at her age, in her grey tweed coat and tartan scarf—of course not! What if they had!

All things shall be well and all manner of things shall be well…

On her way to the bus stop the words sang in her head from long ago, from school and school friends left behind in Ireland years back. You spoke to everyone in Ireland, the part she came from anyway…

The episode on the bench had encouraged her. If you're on your own you're more available to other people—available and vulnerable—yes—both—it was true. She thought of the hard buds on the almond tree holding still against the clear cold sky. *All manner of things shall be well,* she said to herself again.

Better being alone than being with someone you can't talk to—like the man on the bench.

An Experiment in Living
Jenny and June

How cross would you be if someone had eaten the last yogurt in the fridge? Frivolous question, but it needs quite a serious answer if at 64 and 65 respectively you decide to share a house. We, Jenny and June, have had to look at this and a lot of other questions but, because we took a long time to discuss, argue, think and philosophize our way to the final decision to jointly buy our present house, the problem of the last yogurt is very low on our list of priorities.

Probably the most important thing to agree on is the question of a basic philosophy of life. How important are the everyday details of domestic life—and which ones? How much space do you personally need, and is space in the head more important than physical space? Of course, getting the spaces right in the house has been crucial. Totally private sitting rooms, in which we just happen to sleep, and which are entered only by invitation, have proved our greatest boon. Sharing the ground floor, including the kitchen, has given us very few problems. There is a choice of rooms to sit in, quite separately if necessary, with family or friends, and a small garden which suits us both. Two loos, bathroom and separate shower take care of the other basic needs for space. However, the real stroke of genius has been turning the huge basement into a workroom/office. A side bonus has been the way in which our two dogs seem to have managed to sort out their spaces too!

It seems important that anyone who is setting out to share in this way must look carefully at the type of relationship/partnership, call it what you will, that they are entering into. The ability to communicate how each feels about the nuts and bolts of the structure is very important. If there are no-go subjects then the enterprise is doomed. We have found that matters of concern need to be sorted out quickly. If it lingers it will fester! In fact, there have been no major blips because so far we are aware of being in mid-experiment; because some of our friends have expressed considerable apprehension we have tended to regard ourselves as a bit of an experiment.

Perhaps we need to be very sensitive to these doubts—perhaps we should be upfront with these friendly observers. We probably should attempt to explain how we actually work together to integrate securely enough at the fringe to give our separate centers more strength. If we do not develop that strength the enterprise loses meaning. Older people need friends. They do become ill. They do die. Since we are realists, we have tried to write this into our equation so that when disaster strikes we should be able to develop the necessary strategies to meet any contingency.

Needless to say the necessary strategies include good legal advice, preferably from a friendly and sympathetic solicitor like ours. We have a carefully worded Trust Deed which covers our particular requirements. We need to be sure that our respective families will not be left with too many problems. Codicils to Wills take care of what happens to the furniture. We really didn't want arguments about who owned the fridge—never mind the yogurt!—so all movables are joint property.

We couldn't face the thought of trying to synchronize two house sales, particularly in the present state of the property market, so we went ahead with serious house-hunting as soon as one of us had sold. We own the mortgage jointly too; the Building Society was initially startled by two elderly ladies embarking on such a venture but ultimately proved very helpful.

There have been, as always when buying an older house, too many unexpected expenses for us to be able to judge whether we're saving money yet. In theory, we hope to find that living is more economical.

It is, of course, early days. On the whole our families and most of our friends have been polite and apparently approving. We have had to remember that they too need space to maneuver and to make sure that they feel comfortable. Mutual friends haven't necessarily been used to seeing us together, and maybe don't always want to now. Sometimes the kids need mom's shoulder to cry on, ditto friends. So far tact and common sense have helped us avoid problems. Separate telephone lines, plus answering machines, have proved as vital as we had anticipated. For us, sharing a phone would have been a recipe for disaster, maybe others might find different areas of concern.

The "experiment" continues. We have just happily survived a week's holiday together, and it only struck us after we returned that we had actually taken quite a risk! We think we're getting most of it right—so far!

Ellen and Cecile

Not Alone
Anne

I'm all alone, all alone
No sound from the telephone
No friendly voice, not even Joyce
I'm all alone, all alone.

I hear a sound, it is the bell
Who it is I cannot tell
Down the stair, there's no one there
I'm all alone, all alone.

I hear a knock, what a shock
Who at this hour on the clock?
Retrace my steps, Jane perhaps
I'm all alone, all alone.

And there sitting on the mat
As comfy as a pussy-cat
Is a letter. I feel better
I'm not alone, not alone.

A reply from my network link
A questionnaire to make me think
Others are there, my life to share
Women who care, who risk and dare.

I'm not alone, not alone.

CHAPTER SIX

How Can I Deal with What Lies Ahead?

Dear Hen Co-op,

I've always been an active optimistic person but now that I am beginning to feel the limitations of old age and have reached the age when many of my family and friends are dying, I worry about what lies ahead. I realize how precious my life is. How do you deal with this in your lives?

Yours, with best wishes,

Maggie

Dear Maggie,

You are so wise to recognize how precious each moment is, and to want to live it to the full. If you can think of what lies ahead as a continuation of one precious moment after another, then perhaps you can look forward without fear. As you grow older and find yourself becoming less able to do some of the things you want, it will help to focus on what you can do and find the pleasure of the moment in whatever you do.

Life can be difficult as more and more of your family and peers die, and you wonder how you will be able to go on without them. It is important to mourn their loss, to accept your own vulnerability, and to face your own fears. And as Mary says, to tell your family and friends how much they mean to you before it's too late. But it would be destructive to dwell only on the losses without also acknowledging that much in the way of good times and good friends can still lie ahead.

Facing reality about who you are now and how you might be in the future does not mean that you must give up growing old disgracefully. Your disgraceful attitude can help you maintain your optimism, and good friends who are experiencing similar declines can help you keep your sense of humor. When you read Barbara's "Scenes from a Shared Holiday" and Edith's "Parting is Such Sweet Sorrow" you will see how in our group we have had some hilarious moments, talking about hearing loss, stiff limbs, farting unexpectedly, how many pills we take between us, and especially memory loss. Anne, in "On Being Deaf" and "Who's Kidding?" admits to her vulnerability, yet she is able to do so with wry humor. Yes, each of us is experiencing increasing frailty, but together we feel strengthened to cope with whatever lies in store.

One of the most frightening things about contemplating old age is the fear of dependency, especially when you have been active and optimistic, as you say you have been. Having to ask for what you need may seem unfamiliar when you have always been self-sufficient. But asking for what you need is a strength, not a weakness. If you find yourself lonely, ill, frightened, invite a friend for a cup of tea and express your needs to her. Remember how good it feels to be able to help someone else when they need it? Give other people that pleasure, too.

Many of us watch our friends and family members die with the words "if only…" on their lips. Growing old disgracefully means doing as much as you can now, knowing that time is skipping along and pulling us, willy-nilly, with it. To the best of your ability, maintain your interests and stay active. Find people who will stimulate you to try some things you've never tried, and who will expose you to some things you may not have considered, or thought of as impossible. Develop new friendships, try out new activities with an open mind. While new friends are not expected to take the place of the loved ones you have lost, they can be a source of great comfort and enthusiasm, and it may be easier than you think to make new friends as you age. Friendly bit of warning: don't surround yourself with negative-thinking people who will drag you down with their disapproval. There are too many wonderful women who are vital and have positive attitudes about aging for you to hook up with grouches.

In our writings in this chapter, we have tried to show some of the ways we deal with the limitations of old age. We certainly don't have all the answers. None of us knows what lies ahead, nor would we all necessarily want to. We can only trust that our inner resources together with the support and friendship of other women will hold us in good stead as we face whatever is in store.

You are in a transitional time of life. Honor that transition, learn from your setbacks and acknowledge any fear you may have, but also remember that in spite of the seriousness of the issues you might face, there are many more wonderful moments to be had along the way. Keep your sense of humor and find others who will laugh with you. When you are feeling vulnerable, don't be afraid to show it and get the help you need. And, as Sally says, keep living in the here and now and let the future take care of itself.

Disgracefully yours,

The Hen Co-op

Scenes From a Shared Holiday
Barbara
(A true story)

At the breakfast table:

—Have you taken your pills this morning?

—Oh no. Thanks for reminding me. Did you take yours?

—Well, this is the one I take before meals, this one with meals and this one after meals.

—How confusing. Just once a day?

—No. This one is three times a day and this pink one is night and morning. And with the way my memory is going…

Pause

—Damn. Now I can't remember whether I took mine or only thought about taking them. It's lucky they're packed with the days marked— yes, I have taken them.

—Would you like another cup of tea?

—Not if we're going shopping or I'll have to stop and find a loo.

—Can anyone remember what shopping we need?

—Mm, let me think. A lemon?

—A lemon? What did we want a lemon for?

—I don't know. Put it on the list and we might remember what we wanted it for.

—OK. Lemon. What else?

—Milk. Skimmed for Shirley, semi-skimmed for Edith and Anne and Mary, full-cream for Barbara and soy milk for Maxine.

—Butter?

—Oh yes, butter, and margarine for Shirley.

—Coffee decaffeinated for the rest of us but the real stuff for Edith and Barbara. Oh yes, and that grain beverage for Maxine.

—Do we need tea?

—I'll have a look. No, we're OK for ordinary tea but we're getting low on herbal for Anne.

—Right. I think that's all for now. Don't forget your inhaler.

—It's in my bag. How's your ankle this morning?

—Not too bad. How's the back?

—Still there. Not so bad. Let's get going.

In the supermarket car park

—STOP. This is one-way, you're going the wrong way.

—Never mind. Nobody noticed.

—There's a space.

—Too late. Here's another.

—OK. Everybody out.

—Who's got the shopping list?

—Not me.

—Me neither.

—Damn. We must have left it on the table.

—Can anyone remember what we need?

—I know we had a lemon on the list What did we want a lemon for?

Collapse of six old women in helpless laughter.

A Fact of Life
Edith

It happened again today. I try not to believe my own eyes but how can I go on denying the evidence. Why don't I accept the truth when I see it. It's incontrovertible. I have an American cousin who has been warning me about it for years. We used to meet intermittently every few years and whenever I saw her she invariably would work it into the conversation at some point. I don't need her to tell me anymore, I'm accepting what appears to be the inevitable. I'm shrinking! Not only do I have to put up with it but my grandchildren are still growing. It's a complete physical turnaround; now I'm viewed so differently. I have to look up to them, while they look down, down on poor smaller me. IT'S NOT FAIR!

My diminishing height was confirmed again when I was swapping my summer clothes for the winter woollies. It's no longer warm, there's an autumnal chill in the air and in any case it's well after Labor Day. Labor Day is an American holiday, which arrives just a bit later than our August Bank Holiday. In New York, where I was raised, white shoes and all the summer clothes accompanying them were *de trop* after Labor Day, forbidden on pain of…I no longer remember the consequences. At any rate it gave me another good excuse for the change-over. I could stash away the much worn, overwashed, unironed summer apparel and concentrate on the warmer equivalents. In the course of this operation, I decided to try on my ten-year-old little black dress; the one I trot out whenever I feel the occasion demands something more than the usual pair of trousers, and that is what caused the original outburst. It's a loose-fitting affair, no problem with my spreading hips and bulging tummy. Just over the head and down it comes. That's right, down it came. When I looked in the mirror, it looked all wrong. True, I hadn't worn it at all last year, no occasion required it. It couldn't be that I had forgotten how I looked in it. The dress was always a sure winner, except for this very minute. So what was different? I take another look. Of course, it's the length. It's too long. The hem must have come down. My hems are always coming undone. After a careful investigation, I find the hem intact. There was no other explanation; I had shrunk some more. I take off my dress, check my height against the last mark on the cupboard door only to find that I am now almost three inches shorter than I was at my peak.

"It's a fact of life," as one of my granddaughters had no hesitation in telling me. "It happens to women", she went on to explain, "in the postmenopausal period. You can't do anything about it, unless you are on Hormone Replacement Therapy. When the bone density diminishes, as it does, the bone mass decreases," she concluded. Knowing the reason for this unwanted phenomenon doesn't make me feel any better and the knowledge that this process continues just compounds my gloom. I really ought to stop my moaning, just pin up the hem on my dress and see if that improves the overall look.

Old people are just young people trapped inside old bodies.
Nina Bawden

On Being Deaf
Anne

Noise. Isolation.

"What did you say?"

"Thanks for repeating it."

Noise. Moving in a threesome. Shop windows. Christmas candles. Cute cakes. Expensive presents. Narrow pavements. Noise. Isolation.

They're having a conversation. Occasional words drift my way. It's so frustrating. Can I ask her again to repeat what she's saying? She doesn't mind, but I get fed up with asking.

What if it gets worse? Oh no, I can't bear to think how it will be if it gets worse. How to communicate? With a smile? In writing? Learn sign language? I pray it will never be as bad as that.

They are very considerate. Sit or stand on the right side by my good ear. But I find it tiresome, frustrating. I do a little dance to get myself into place to hear better.

I must remain pleasant, contented. It's so boring to whine and moan. Am I a bore? Would I feel bored if someone else kept saying "I can't hear you," "what did you say?," "it's so noisy in here," or "everywhere we go is noisy." Yes, I probably would be bored. How boring to be boring. How boring to be deaf.

I'm not going to let it stop me enjoying the company of my friends. I will avoid noisy surroundings, or at least not try to maintain a conversation on crowded streets.

The Survivors
Mary

I have a twin sister. She is the dearest person on earth to me, not count-ing my children. It is unbearable to think of one of us still existing in the world without the other.

And yet sooner or later, one of us will have to face that situation …with the death of the person we have been closest to all our lives. I do not know how people can survive such grief—and yet they do.

Everyone who survives into old age must wonder like this about the future, for themselves and the friends and family they love—who will go first, how will they manage alone…?

Survivors must survive on memories—treasured memories like the ones I have of my mother. When I first left home to join the Women's Land Army, every spring she sent me snowdrops, posted in an old red OXO tin, with their stems wrapped carefully in damp moss to keep them fresh.

I treasure those memories of her, especially the memories of the snowdrops. Every spring, when I first see snowdrops I think of her.

And I wonder how it will be for me…

Such memories are precious, sweet and painful at the same time. And it's hard to talk about things like this while the people we love are still alive.

Eve, one of my oldest and dearest friends had two serious heart operations recently. She wrote farewell letters to all the people she loved—just in case.

Dear Eve! I'm so glad you didn't go. I want to tell you how much I love you and how lonely I would have been without you, especially in those days when we were next-door neighbors. It was not long after the end of the War. We had both married and moved to a strange city. We were hard up, tied to the house with small children—seven between us!

We sat together on the back step every summer for hours in the sun and talked, while the babies slept in their baby carriages and the older children built play houses with mats and old curtains on the lawn.

On Friday evenings we took the children with us to the rummage sale at the church hall. Then, when we got home we couldn't wait to get dressed up in our new finery. We had picnics together and wonderful (cheap!) Halloween and New Year's Eve and Burns' Night parties...

Eve told me about her childhood in Scotland with five sisters and three brothers, how they had had to sit and polish the apples at night ready for her Dad to take out with the horse and cart on his round in the morning. About her youngest and favorite sister who married a New Zealand airman during the War and she sailed away from Scotland forever, how he left her homeless with four children, and how she was befriended by a Maori family.

I got to know Eve and all her family so well, it was as if I'd lived a second life!

Now that I am 70 I think I need to tell my family and friends how important they have been in my life, how much I love them and depend on them for my present sense of well-being.

It's easy to leave these things unsaid—but we cannot know for certain who are to be the survivors—or when. I would like to think that when the time comes, survivor or not, all the loving thoughts still waiting in my heart will have been said.

I would like to collect all these precious memories together, and many more, like daisies to make a chain, or beads to thread on a necklace, and live them through again one by one and to speak a blessing of love on all the people who share these memories with me.

Talk in the Dark
Mary

In the dark like now
Are you afraid?

In the end like now
Are you afraid?

Bring in the roses
Set them down
Against the sky

Step for the dancing
Take my hand
Wreathing the sky

Bring love with you
Arms around me
Then tell me true

In the dark like now
Are you afraid?

At My Mother's Funeral
Maxine

I wrote this when my mother died and I realized that with both parents gone, I had taken their place at the edge of the cliff. There was no buffer left for me. I experienced terror as I glimpsed, for a brief moment, how it really was for me to recognize my own mortality. I also felt the exhilaration of that release.

I am clinging to a thin, swaying fragile tree on the jagged edge of a cliff; a violent, sharp wind is terrorizing the twig to which I have anchored myself; my skin is stripped away; I feel everything: the shapes, textures, sizes, color, smells are all blindingly clear. I feel the sharpness of the tree's bark, the serrated edge of the cliff, the wind-knife slashing my every nerve-ending.

No one else exists. I cannot let go of the branch to grab a hand, a tree, a rock because there is nothing and no one except the wind and me. I know that the twig must give way, will give way. I will try to plant myself in the earth, ground myself in whatever I can experience as tangible, knowing all the while that soon I will be swept tumbling and weightless into a feared and fearful void beyond the precipice. I am next in line.

I am alive for the first time, existing in a most thrilling, free, mortal wholeness. I am also raw fear, facing my mortality as a curse placed upon me, a demon-monkey on my back that I never asked for. All sensations are at once: thrill and fear, impotence and power, sadness and joy. I want to freeze the moment and hold on to it in all its pain and pleasure. I want to let go of it, deaden it, erase it and pretend that the world is back for me in all its discrete, knowable and manageable parts.

I slowly reassemble the skins and cushions and blankets and walls and ceilings and veils and rational thoughts and wrap myself in them.

The long sleeves of these, my protections, stop the wind from touching my body, but I am aware of it being there, just barely out of reach, still within the boundaries of my consciousness, teasing and threatening and promising. It is my freedom and my tormentor.

> The years seem to rush by now, and I think of death as a fast approaching end of a journey—double and treble reasons for loving as well as working while it is day.
> *George Eliot*

Platitudes and Other Unhelpful Remarks on the Death of a Loved One

Anne

How useful people find those automatic responses when meeting some-one recently bereaved.

"I was so shocked to hear of your sad loss."
(Yes, I expect you were. So how do you think I feel?)

"My dear husband has just died."
"No, I don't believe it."
(This is not what I need to hear.)

"I feel terrible. My pet dog has just been run over."
"Yes, I know how you feel. I must tell you about the sad incident when I lost my cat."
(Please listen to me. I don't want to listen to you.)

How one longs for silence, for empathetic listening, perhaps even "I'm so sorry." The traditional Jewish condolence which I grew up with, "I wish you long life," can feel totally inappropriate when you are feel-ing that you don't want to live on without your deceased beloved, and you are certainly not in the right frame of mind to consider a long life on your own after so many years of wedded happiness.

With your mind, body and spirit staggering under the burden of sadness, guilt, love, relief and many other mixed feelings, you don't want someone to discuss with you in every detail and particular the food and drink for after the funeral.

(Yes, normally I like to be consulted but now please do what you think best, and don't continue to burden me with what feel like irrelevancies.)

C. S. Lewis says, at the beginning of his moving book *A Grief Observed*, "I find it hard to take in what anyone says. Or perhaps, hard to want to take it in…If only they would talk to one another and not to me."

"How will you manage?"
"Will you stay in your present home?"
"What shall we do with the clothes?"
(Give me time. Give me space. Let me protect myself from outside battering. I know you mean well. Let me relive in my thoughts, our love, our relationship, our differences, our difficulties. Let me be myself, on my own, myself without her, myself cut off from him.)

I think the words I want to hear are "I wish you peace."

Sadness

Barbara

I am a strong woman, a survivor.
I organize my life, pay the bills,
Run a car, know my way around,
Manage my finances,
Keep the show on the road,
Love my friends, as they love me,
Read good books, see the latest films,
Enjoy music, from classical to jazz,
And good food and my daily tot of Scotch,
Love my kids, adore my grandchildren.
It sounds a great life.
Why then do I sometimes feel
Such cosmic sadness in my soul?

Life Isn't Fair
Sally

Being old conjures up for me pictures of my body not doing what I would like it to do, bodily functions behaving in ways that I don't expect and don't like; of having choices of what I can do with my life reduced and restricted. If this is a definition, then parts of me have been old for a long time.

I felt old when, walking home from the local station, a five minute walk away, I had to sit down on a seat and garden walls several times, clung to hedges and bushes for support, fell twice before I made it to my front door and the whole journey took nearly half an hour—and I was then 34. I felt old the day my husband bought a walking stick and virtually ordered me to use it—I should have used one for months before. I must have looked old when I, in a wheelchair, my husband and a British Rail guard waited for the Newcastle to London train and the guard, looking at Jim, asked me, "Is your son coming with yer?" I felt old when, having mentioned to the district nurse that I was having bladder incontinence problems, she produced the largest pair of plastic underpants I had ever seen—the kind my three-year-old daughter had recently stopped using—and suggested that "These would help, dear." When I exploded saying that I didn't want to crackle when I sat down, she agreed that they didn't really fit the bill for a 32-year-old.

Let me explain a little. I worked as a social worker for five years, married, had a baby daughter and did all the sort of things that were expected of a young, healthy woman. When I was 32, all the strange feelings and bodily malfunctions that I had been experiencing since shortly after Rosie was born, were diagnosed as multiple sclerosis or MS for short.

MS is a disease of the central nervous system and consequently can affect many different body functions. In addition, the course and prognosis of the disease is unknown so no one could tell me if I would deteriorate, how fast that would be and so I, my husband and daughter faced an unknown and very frightening future. Now 25 years later I know that mine was the slow deteriorating sort and my worst fears have not been realized—yet. With the degree of disability that I have now, I can lead a very full and independent life.

But let me go back even further to when I was born with the congenital condition of Albinism. This lack of pigmentation affects the retina of the eye and I was only partially sighted. So when my MS was diagnosed, I had already had plenty of experience of being a bit different, of having to make excuses why I couldn't do certain things like play tennis, of having to use public transport because I couldn't hold a driving license, or recognize people in the street until I was close to them. I felt I had had my share of disability yet here was another one to contend with. It wasn't fair—which of course it wasn't but then life isn't fair and anyone who thinks it is has a hard time.

These two conditions juxtaposed in me raise the question of whether it is better to be born with a disability and so never know any different or to have one imposed upon you as an adult so that you know what you are missing. But these two situations cannot be judged as better or worse, they are just different and it is impossible to put a value on either. Both are a challenge for the person concerned. I still long to walk on the open moorland with streams and springy heather to find total solitude but I am happy when willing family or friends push me as far as they are able and then leave me while they walk further.

For years I have had to keep my mouth shut when people getting off the floor with some difficulty say, "This is what happens to you when you get old." People almost twice my age hold doors open for me. I read with envy of outings, holidays, places to go that I know are out of the question using a wheelchair. I have had to turn my back on aspects of life which would be impossible to get to or achieve and make the most of what I CAN do. But I also have to think carefully about whether in fact I COULD do something with a bit more of an adventurous spirit and taking some risks. I have done many things: I have been to Greece several times, Morocco, Egypt and India, taken a degree. I am involved in many local activities and lead a full and interesting life. But it requires that I make the most of what I have got rather than lamenting what I haven't. So easy to say and so difficult to do at times.

So I feel that one way or another I have had a lifetime of adjusting to a restricted lifestyle, of facing an unknown future, of making the most of what I have—isn't that what people have to do as they get older and their capacity and life changes? I've been doing it for years. So for me aging will just be another boulder in the path of life which requires some initiative to overcome and I shall observe with interest how my contemporaries adjust to my sort of lifestyle. But one of the additional problems is that my friends and relations are getting older alongside me and where ten years ago they were quite willing and capable of pushing me to the top of Haworth Moor, the flesh and the spirit are now less willing and so their reduced energy must also be mine. With my kind of deteriorating MS and the process of aging, I will find it more and more difficult to walk and be independent. That conjures up all sorts of unpleasant images like needing help to get up and go to bed, help with washing and lavatory, lots of areas where my independence would be severely eroded and questions of who would do it and will I lose my fighting spirit? I have never been very patient at the best of times. These changes are a very real possibility and are likely to come sooner rather than later. All the more reason to keep living in the here and now and not think about it too much. So it is up to me to keep up the exercises, keep muscles going as long as possible and above all keep a positive and good-humored attitude. Let the future look after itself.

Parting is Such Sweet Sorrow
Edith

I think I may have come up with another taboo subject, not to be discussed in either mixed or single-sex groups and certainly not a topic for dinner conversation. The old taboos of sex and death are fast fading, especially now that it's "sex rampant" in all the glossy magazines, every aspect minutely explored. A replacement is well overdue. I may have found it!

It was when I was in New York recently with a few women I had known during my protracted college period. We had barely kept in touch and hadn't seen much of one another over the years, but when one of them heard I was visiting New York, a mini reunion was arranged. We went through the usual range of topics, starting with a run-through on what we had been doing as well as an acknowledgment of where we were now. Eventually, health "at our time of life" came onto the agenda. Some common physical problems surfaced; experiences as well as suggested remedies were exchanged. We had pretty much exhausted the subject when a general lull in the conversation occurred. I took the opportunity of mentioning one of my concerns by asking whether farting was a problem for anyone. Diana, who was sitting opposite, looked puzzled and wondered aloud why "parting" was a problem. "Is it when somebody near and dear to you leaves, or is it when you go but would really rather stay, or is there gossip about a marriage breakup I haven't yet heard about?" When Diana had finished, I explained that she had misheard and enunciating clearly, I restated my difficulty, "It's 'farting' I'm asking about, not 'parting'." Dead silence. I went on to define it more simply, "It's the passing or breaking of wind." Still no reaction. I continued, hoping that when I explained my situation, I'd get some feedback. "It has something to do with muscular control," I continued. "It seems that as we age the muscles weaken so the control diminishes. There have been a few embarrassing occasions when I didn't manage to leave the room in time. My grandchildren have no hesitation in saying 'someone has made a pooh' and then looking directly at me, naming no names of course." I was expecting general recognition and suggestions for my condition from my hitherto silent audience, but none came, only embarrassed silence, interrupted quickly by someone posing a question about one of her grandchildren. I accepted defeat. My subject abruptly terminated. Nobody wished to acknowledge that problem, even if it did exist.

I wonder if it's a question of terminology. Is there another word that could be substituted for "farting"? Perhaps "parting" isn't so far out. It would be short for "parting with wind." Or possibly an award-winning competition could be held to choose a new word to describe the process, or perhaps a French expression to give it cachet and mystery. The trouble is I'm still left with an unsolved problem. Not a suggestion in sight.

Thanks for the Memory
Barbara

As Noel Coward said, "Strange how potent cheap music is." As we grow older the more loudly and insistently those potent songs of our youth play in our heads. The fact that we six Hens are all in the same age group gives us a common background of popular music and hardly a conversation passes without a remark triggering the memory of a song (but that was long ago and now my dum-de-dum-dum is but the memory of a song). And we are off, in a less than harmonious, ragged chorus. Some of us know the words but can't sing in tune (Maxine and Edith both claim that this is because they were told as children that they couldn't sing in tune and have believed it ever since). Others hum along because they can't remember the words.

When we start discussing our writing, every theme seems to lead us to a whole new range of songs. One song leads to another, it's amazing how easily we find ways to avoid getting down to writing.

Now we are discussing themes for this chapter, commiserating with each other on our failing faculties. I feel a parody coming on, to the tune of "Thanks for the Memory" (with apologies to lyricist Leo Robin).

Oh, where's my memory?
I used to be so great
At remembering every date
And everybody's number—I'd never hesitate
But now it's all gone!

Oh, where's my memory?
What was it you just said?
It's vanished from my head

While I remember things you said ten years ago instead.
Oh where has it gone?

I make lists as well as I'm able
Then leave them behind on the table.
My mind's like the Tower of Babel,
Connections blown
And facts all flown.

So, where is my memory?
It's really such a bore
To start to tell once more
The anecdotes you've told your friends a hundred times before.
Awfully glad I met you
But, pardon me, what is your name?
—I've forgotten so much!

Happiness is good health and a bad memory.
Ingrid Bergman

Spices and Immortality
Maxine

Other people have said that they perceive me as being almost insufferably well-organized, which of course is how I would like to be. In fact, I spend a great deal of time setting up files, making cataloguing systems, arranging and rearranging drawers and shelves, setting shoes in neat rows, color-coding labels, and alphabetizing spice jars, to name but a few of my attempts. Then I proceed to throw bits and pieces of paper into undesignated files, leaving empty the lovely color-coded file folders. Shoes are dropped on top of one another. About the only sacred system is the spice jar rack. Woe be unto anyone who puts paprika where oregano belongs.

Was I always this interested in order? I remember that as a child I tried to keep my toys and clothes in perfect condition, probably due to the fact that I grew up poor during the Great Depression years, when there was a need to preserve precious possessions because they were not easily replaceable. My sister, on the other hand, was born five years after me, and was a different sort of person. She seemed to destroy something just by looking at it. Nothing was left intact when she got hold of it, and that included my toys. My prized possession was a Shirley Temple doll with beautiful hair and long curls, acquired for me at great parental sacrifice. I kept her in pristine condition. Rosalee decided that she could improve the doll's appearance by giving her a haircut. Shirley's curls were lost along with all her clothes. I still have the naked, bareheaded remains, tucked safely in a storage box, a mute reminder of my dear sister who died very young, still disorganized, while I am still trying to put everything in order with less than perfect results. It is my attempt at immortality.

There is a story I remember from way back (I think it was by O. Henry) in which a young girl is very ill. From her bed she is watching the autumn leaves fall from the trees. She vows she will live as long as there is even one leaf left. Someone who loves her comes and paints a leaf on the window, and thinking that it is still on the tree, her determination to live goes on.

I feel that way about my organizational attempts. There always has to be one more project before I can die. So I continue to throw bits of paper into piles with an eye to finding just the right place for them later. If I did not have these scattered piles, I might die.

Irrational, of course, and I am well aware of my mortality, but it is fun to look for reasons to reject it. It is as good an excuse as any for my unsorted papers, when I have such a strong tendency to be compulsively organized.

There are those who say that astrology has the answer: I organize because my sun sign is Virgo, but Sagittarius rising balances out the tendencies, and my moon in Cancer gives me a need to continually remake my nest. Hmmm. I suppose that is as good an explanation as any, but whatever the reason, I shall enjoy my alphabetized spices while I go on searching for immortality.

A Shared Life??
Edith

Recently I found myself watching a documentary about a widowed woman attempting to come to terms with her altered situation. Her husband had obviously been totally in charge of every aspect of her life, including the financial. In consequence, she was unprepared for what followed. Her unscrupulous son stepped in to fill the gap, took charge and she was left ultimately without any resources.

It is not an uncommon story: many husbands not only take charge of the purse strings but do not discuss money matters with their spouses. This is probably less so in the case of working wives where more equitable arrangements operate. I can, however, remember an exception to that when a friend of mine, who admittedly worked only intermittently, was becoming concerned about her husband's impending retirement. She had no real knowledge of their financial position and was worried about the future when there would be no regular income; nor was she aware of any arrangements for an additional pension besides the state one. Each time she tried to communicate her anxieties about the future, he would offer her general reassurance, explaining that as he was looking after things there was no need to worry. This reply did nothing to allay her anxieties. She needed factual information of what lay ahead. It was when all her efforts had failed that she came to me for help. She wondered whether my husband over lunch with her husband would be able to elicit some positive information in that area.

It sounds ridiculous that in a shared life, frequently over long periods, one important part of it should remain shrouded in mystery. When I was recounting this ludicrous story to another friend, I was surprised to learn that she was in the same position and was quite content not to know. When I asked "why not?," she said she didn't want to know. As her husband was looking after things that was enough for her. I find it difficult to understand that attitude but then I suppose many women of my generation never had the relevant experience of managing their own finances. We were socialized to believe that after marriage (the ultimate goal in women's lives), the "Living Happily Ever After" contained an understanding that her spouse would now be responsible for her debts, or words to that effect. I can only imagine that many women never questioned this arrangement and were content to be looked after.

I was raised in a totally different household, where it was my mother who was in charge of the finances as it was she who kept us afloat during my father's long period of unemployment. I just picked up from that; given the choice of managing what remained of my ten dollar a week wage, after a good part of it had gone into the housekeeping fund, or letting my mother do it for me, I opted for the former and never looked back. However, it must be more difficult for women in long-term relationships who have never worked to bring the same know-how or willingness to share the ups and downs of the family finances. It is a situation that many women may have to face one day as more of them outlive their male partners. If they are inexperienced and unequipped to pick up the financial reins whether by choice or not, they are going to have a difficult time. So along with the Girl Guides, my advice is: "Be Prepared."

Who's Kidding?—More Reflections On an Aging Body and Mind
Anne

Some people say that as you get older you cannot do all the things that you were able to do in youth and middle age. I regard that as nonsense. I am as fit and supple as ever. My body is agile, my mind is sharp, my skin glows, my teeth glisten, my eyes sparkle.

Of course it is more difficult to actually see my eyes as they disappear into deeper and deeper pouches. Conversely you can see much more of my teeth as the gums gradually recede. My skin now forms an interesting network of lines like the surface of a lake rippled by the wind, or like clouds in a mackerel sky.

I'm as active as ever. Why, this very morning I shopped in the busy marketplace. It took me twice as long as it used to, but so what, I wasn't in any hurry. Of course, I then sank gratefully onto the settee to listen to the afternoon play on the radio. Well, why not, I've retired and can spend my time as I want. It was an excellent play. To be truthful, it had an excellent beginning and an exciting finish, but I rather missed out on what happened in the middle. The BBC should be more considerate and give a quick resume after about twenty minutes for those who need a quick catnap in the middle of the day.

I can beat any youngster at snap, dominoes, snakes and ladders or go fish, as long as they are under seven. I'm still a great bridge-player. I know I do sometimes mishear the calls, drop the cards, see hearts instead of diamonds, but that just makes the game more interesting for everyone.

I no longer run for buses. It seems pointless because, until I get right up close I can't see whether it's the number I want or not. And what about getting on and off the bus—they seem to be making the steps higher and higher. It's fun being a "Twerly" though. That's somebody who has a free bus pass, but can't use it until after nine o'clock because it's too early. I'm always surprised when the driver looks at it and just nods. You would think he would say, "Hey, you—you can't use that, you're not old enough," but they have never questioned it.

It's good to know that nothing changes. Well, I don't feel any older anyway!

Mimi

Losing My Marbles
Shirley

Red and shiny, it was knocked by the green one to the left, continuing on its surprise journey under the sofa, out of sight.

"I've lost my marble," cried my granddaughter.

We went down on our hands and knees, rummaging beneath the sofa, pulling out bits of fluff, a pencil or two, shopping lists long out of date. No marble was to be seen. So we impatiently pulled the seat from its usual position and there it was. No longer shiny but covered with dust and the remains of cobwebs. A quick wash brought back the glow to the shiny glass ball and a welcome brush and pan job rectified the accumulated dirt.

That marble was easier to retrieve and return to its pristine condition than the marbles I've lost and continue to lose. I hit my forehead with the palm of my hand as if to jolt all the loose pieces back into place in my head. I'm certainly losing my marbles. My brain just won't work as I want it to. I can't even remember names of faces that are very familiar. Someone told me that she rang a friend, but when the receiver was picked up at the other end, she couldn't remember her own name! The ultimate degradation. That has not happened to me yet but, in my dreams, I forget my telephone number and often get lost, spending the nightmare searching for a home I can't find or recognize.

I lose my keys constantly and have wild panic attacks while my already high blood pressure soars further, as I search through my many pockets. I often put things in special safe places so that I'll remember where they are, but of course when I come to it, I don't.

I start doing something, then the phone rings and I'll be darned if I can remember what it was I was doing before. I have lists everywhere of things to do today, tomorrow, next week but can never find them when I want them. I write to people then do so again, forgetting that

I've already done that, then ignore others. At the grocer's, I frequently come home with more almond essence. I knew there was some cooking ingredient I needed but can never remember which, so that there are now about a dozen bottles of essence on my shelf but no vanilla, which is what I really need. How can I polish my marbles, keep them from running away? Constant use helps prevent the panic at losing them all, but they certainly seem to run further and further from my reach, even though the throw is sluggish. Maybe I should take up ten-pin bowling instead. At least the pins are easier to see and someone else picks them up!

> **The old are the invisible minority…but they do have the power to menace us with our own inevitable futures.**
> *Mary Gordon*

CHAPTER SEVEN

So What Do You Do That's Disgraceful?

Dear Hens,

I enjoyed reading your book and felt quite excited by some of your ideas but I'd like to know what exactly you mean when you write about growing old disgracefully. I feel the need to make some changes in my life but I am a little anxious about the reactions I might get from my friends and family. How do I start?

With best wishes,

Liz

Dear Liz,

In our first book, when we were defining what growing old disgracefully means to us, we used the expression "it's my turn now" to try to give women a way of thinking about what we meant. We stressed the idea of letting go of the "shoulds" and "oughts" that many of us have lived with during our lifetimes of service to everyone except ourselves. We also tried to make clear that growing old disgracefully may not be for everyone, or may mean something quite different to others, depending on their circumstances. To quote from Chapter 4 of *Growing Old Disgracefully*:

> There are no universal recipes or prescriptions, for what is a challenge to one woman may appear perfectly safe, even mundane, to another.

Throughout both our books, our writings reflect our ways of looking at the world, which are certainly not the only ways. We have tried to share the changes that have come about in our lives as a result of meeting each other, writing two books together, and nurturing our connections to each other. We have found that the support of other women is essential in maintaining a positive attitude towards aging, and we have watched as the Growing Old Disgracefully Network has grown and flourished, giving an opportunity for more and more women to find their web of friendships.

Our definition of growing old disgracefully suggests the opposite of growing old gracefully, which to us means having to live out your life passively and unnoticed. While we do not consider ourselves a political group in the usual sense of the word, we definitely have the hope that if enough women decide to grow old disgracefully, together we can challenge the stereotypes of old women and refuse to accept agism in its many forms. We believe that women can start from wherever they are to take small steps toward a richer, more rewarding and definitely more fun-filled life.

Most of us have been taught that as adults we should be serious and dignified, and leave the playing to children. The rule we learned is "Act Your Age!" But one of the great advantages of growing old disgracefully is letting go of other people's rules. As Edith says in "Seventy-six Trombones," it is a great feeling of release to let yourself go, to sing, dance, play games, or whatever takes your fancy, without worrying about what someone else might think. Reactivating the playful, creative child that is still within us is essential to our definition.

Shirley points out that learning to accept your own imperfections can free up a lot of energy to spend on growing old disgracefully. But it can also lead to a kind of complacency, so it is important to decide for yourself what things, if any, you want to change about yourself or your life, then find allies to help you through the changes. The main point is that it is you who will make those decisions, not someone else.

In the following pieces, we have tried to show how our lives have been affected by the decision to grow old disgracefully. There are many more stories to be told, possibly much different from ours. Each person who liberates herself from the demands she finds restrictive, each one who finds a way to assert her own needs and desires, every woman who says "it's my turn now" and embarks on a path of new or deferred adventures—each of these helps to create the definition of what it means to grow old disgracefully.

We hope you find our writings helpful in coming up with your own meanings, and that you will discover your own ways to age with enthusiasm.

Sincerely,

The Hen Co-op

My Disgraceful Old Age
Barbara

"So, Barbara, what do you do that's disgraceful?"

This is not an easy question to answer. Life is not always wonderful, full of joy and laughter. Growing older is not always fun. I certainly have not got all the answers. But I do know that the philosophy of growing old disgracefully has changed the way I think about myself and relate to the people around me.

My generation of women grew up before the Women's Movement raised women's consciousness, shaking them out of their passive acceptance of male dominance. Most young women today do not see themselves as passive and marginalized, waiting to find their identity and to live their lives through the "real" lives of their strong, active, male partners. They know that there are other alternatives even if they still, in the main, choose the conventional path. We older women have a lot to learn from them. But we think that they also have a lot to learn from us, because many of us have found the strength to reject our conditioning, to find our separate identities and to tell our own stories, recognizing that we have stories worth telling. Even if our first book had not been published, we six Hens had all been changed by the experience of working together on writing it. Through examining and writing about our lives we began to have a better understanding of ourselves and were able to look back on our younger selves with tenderness and compassion.

So, my first emphatic answer to the question which heads this piece is "I write." I now describe myself as a writer and that feels good and powerful. Sometimes I write through tears, sometimes smiling to myself. Sometimes I am amazed and delighted by what I have written—more often I tear it up and try again. Writing my story and sharing it with other women (in fact, with thousands of other women since the publication of our first book) has been the most exciting and "disgraceful" activity of my old age. Writing your own story and sharing it with other women is not mere self-indulgence, it is liberating and empowering. You find the common threads which run through women's lives and acknowledge the strengths you have needed to deal with the pains and difficulties along the way.

This brings me to my second answer. When I was first on my own after years of being part of a couple, just "me," no longer "we," nearly all my friends were in couples. They were kind and loving but I often felt like a poor relation because my need was so much greater than theirs. Over the years, in addition to these old, dear friends, I have found a large circle of friends who are also alone and with whom I can enjoy meals, films, music, walking or just being, on an equal footing. Friends are an essential ingredient of a disgraceful old age. As we have often said, you cannot be properly disgraceful on your own.

But, despite the writing and the friends there are inevitably some bad times as you grow old living alone and we all need to devise some survival strategies for dealing with those bad times. So here are some that help me. They are really just plain common sense, nothing very profound but they might be helpful to you if your life has changed and you are facing a new situation.

• I have cultivated a taste for solitude. In the past, days on my own always made me feel sad and lonely but I have learned to relish being alone, moving at my own pace, eating when and what I feel like eating. I enjoy the silence and space to think and the freedom of choice.

• Acknowledging that a whole blank week in my diary depresses me, I plan ahead so that I have some dates to look forward to when solitude begins to pall.

• The telephone is a lifeline, not a luxury but an essential element of life as I grow old. A call to a distant friend, however short, reminds me that we care about each other and if we lived near enough to meet we might spend more than the cost of the call. So I always budget to allow myself this pleasure.

• I dress for comfort and to please myself. I do sometimes dress up when I feel like dressing up but I absolutely refuse to wear uncomfortable shoes!

• I constantly, and consciously, relish the minor pleasures life offers and the bonus of having the time to enjoy them. Reading in bed in the morning, walking across the park picking up shiny horse chestnuts, doing the crossword by the window in my cosy sitting room while I watch others rush off to work, wandering through Kew Gardens in the rain with a dear friend, sharing meals and laughter. Small pleasures which weave into the tapestry of a well-lived life.

• I am not marking time until the next stage. Who knows what the next stage might be? I am choosing to live in the here and now, making the most of everything and open to every new opportunity.

Nothing very profound, as I said. Just a positive attitude, a shift of perception, not a major revolution. But I have saved for last the most important element of our independent, free old age. And that is laughter and a sense of fun. In our first book we wrote of our discovery of the power of shared laughter, it helps us to give each other the strength to change the ways in which we think of ourselves. I know now that I will not be content to be a little old lady, waiting on the sidelines, dwindling down into death. I am, and will be, a powerful old woman, growing old disgracefully through good times and bad.

> **In the end, the changed life for women will be marked, I feel certain, by laughter…it is the laughter of women together that is the revealing sign, the spontaneous recognition of insight and love and freedom.**
> *Carolyn Heilbrun*

Just Watch!
Maxine

In our previous book, *Growing Old Disgracefully*, I wrote in my short autobiography that early in life, like a chameleon, I learned to take on the protective coloration of those around me in order to feel safe and accepted. I developed an inner life where I could try out my thoughts and feelings without letting anyone else in on them. I doubt that I will ever completely lose that fear of ridicule and rejection, but little by little I am learning to let others know me as myself, rather than as a version that might please them more. I hope that the people I care about will like and accept me, but if not, my ego will still be intact. I find this very liberating, a major difference in who I am now as opposed to how I started out. It is part of what I am doing these days to grow old as disgracefully as I can.

What else am I doing? It is difficult to pinpoint specific examples; it is more a change of attitude. Even though I have frequently shocked polite society in the past, there was always a slight feeling of guilt or fear of going too far. Now I find it much easier to be bold. Take last week, for instance. My friend and I stopped for lunch at a self-service deli. We took our food to the cashier's station but found no one there. After a reasonable wait, I decided that if they couldn't have someone there to take our money, we could jolly well take our food outside without paying. We had a lovely picnic, and contrary to what I would have done in the past, we did not go back to search for the cashier. Theft? Well, perhaps, but I consider it a protest against poor service, as well as a statement of support for the working class: if businesses would employ more people, instead of exploiting the few, there would be an extra cashier.

I no longer assume that everything is my fault. If a film that I suggested turns out to be a dud, I blame it on the filmmakers, and I do not feel I have to apologize. I remember feeling as if it were my fault if it rained on a day when an outing was planned. (My dear friend Virginia, who died a few years ago, used to swear that her mother-inlaw blamed her for World War II.)

I no longer consider silence a virtue. Speaking up is OK, and speaking up louder is even better in some cases. Along with this, I have found it much easier to ask for what I need, although that is still somewhat problematic for me.

I am much more comfortable dancing when and where I fancy, even in a group of much younger people. If they are put off by it, then they need to work on their own attitudes. I don't need to stop dancing to make them more comfortable. I have not quite got to that point with singing, however.

I ask for tastes of food before I buy, and I send unsatisfactory meals back in restaurants. I ask to speak to supervisors or managers when someone tells me that something cannot be done or "it's the rules." I do not always get desired results, but at least I know I tried.

These are but a few examples of how my new growing old disgracefully persona manifests. I may not do something outrageous each and every day, but I know I could if I wanted to. And I will, you can bet on it. Just watch!

The more you praise and celebrate your life, the more there is in life to celebrate.
Oprah Winfrey

I've Said I'm Sorry
Mary

It's too easy saying sorry
I've got a lot to learn!
I've just said sorry to the cat—
It's someone else's turn!

I've said sorry to the postman
And to the milkman too
Cos he forgot to leave the milk!
Can you believe that's true?

I'm always getting pushed aside
When I'm getting on the bus
And then I say I'm sorry
And I don't make any fuss.

"Now you, girl, say you're sorry!"
That's what women had to learn.
But now that I am old and bold
It's someone else's turn!

Social Constraints
Anne

When I was eight, my Uncle George invited me to his warehouse to choose a doll for my birthday. I entered a large room lined with shelves and on those shelves were row upon row of dolls. Small, unclothed dolls sat and stood, shiny and bare under the overhead lights. Clothed, medium-sized dolls in cotton dresses, fur-trimmed capes or wool cardigans. Dolls in sailor-suits, dolls in pajamas, blond dolls, brunette dolls, dolls with straight hair and dolls with curly hair. Dolls with red-dimpled smiling faces, dolls with sallow serious faces, with blue eyes or brown eyes.

Looking higher, my eyes alighted on a large doll, wearing a pink crinoline dress, trimmed with lace. She wore a bonnet on her fair, curling hair and she returned my admiring gaze with blue eyes and dark curved lashes.

Uncle George followed me round the room, watching my excited glances and asked me which doll I would like. I was about to claim the doll in the pink crinoline to be my very own when a small voice in my head told me that to choose that prize would be greedy and quite unacceptable. My well-developed conscience and my real longing battled for several minutes before I chose the medium-sized cherub sitting on the shelf at my eye level. Without question, she was put into my waiting arms and subsequently well cared for in my doll's pram and in my homely games of mothers-and-fathers, but I always yearned passionately for the crinolined beauty gazing from on high.

Now that I am a disgraceful old woman I have put aside all social constraints. If invited I can go into a restaurant and choose the most expensive dish. I adore and request the most luxurious chocolates with crisp mint centers and dark bitter covering.

I have to admit that I am rarely asked to choose from a room full of priceless gifts, but, if the chance ever comes to me again, I will choose the one I want even if it is the largest, best and costs the earth!

Seventy-six Trombones
Edith

What would anyone coming up to their seventy-sixth birthday want for a present? I was just waiting to be asked. When that question did come up, there was no need for me to give it any thought. "Seventy-six Trombones," I replied without a moment's hesitation.

I was in California at the time with some members of our writing group, having joined them for readings to publicize the American edition of our book. There I would be for my birthday, a long way from home and my immediate family. What could have been a stressful time for me, turned out to be completely otherwise. It was a glorious day from start to finish. The early mist cleared on our drive to Monterey. Warm sunshine and a clear blue sky were to be the backdrop for *my* day. Imagine me in the company of whales, elasmobranchii (sharks to you), fishes of all shapes and colors including the memorable Moon Jelly, this beautiful, translucent member of the better known Jellyfish family. There they were at the Monterey Bay Aquarium, just waiting to wish me a Happy Birthday. This was a whole new experience in birthday celebrations and once back at Maxine's, there was more to come. Lots of wonderful surprises: flowers, telephone calls from England, cards, very, very special presents, and amongst them by special request…my *seventy-six trombones*. Yes, my wish had been granted! There they were locked up in a recording of the "Music Man" where they had always been, in the collection of songs from that musical. The record, as we were later to discover, was in pristine condition, possibly never played before. We did have to wait to hear it until our return to England, since Maxine's advanced equipment wasn't able to handle this thirty-year-old recording.

What a welcoming reception those trombones eventually received in London. It was already a special occasion since all six of us had come to be together: Maxine from California, Mary from Stockton, joining with the four Londoners. I put on the record and when my seventy-six trombones came on playing *my song*, my living room suddenly erupted. Each of us, picking up whatever was on hand for keeping time with the music, started to move, accompanying the rhythm with our improvised instruments. Our movements took over; as we danced we pushed the furniture aside to create as much space as possible. We danced separately, in a line, holding hands, twirling arms, legs and bodies on the move, always keeping time to the specific beat of the music. It's hard to describe that feeling of utter release and exhilaration when you let yourselves go and we certainly did that. It was frenetic; it was exhausting; it was such fun. We all collapsed laughing when it was over. I certainly had my seventy-six trombones with a vengeance. It's not over yet since I can put them on at any time, especially when I feel low, just conjure up a picture of not-so-long-ago, turn myself on and *dance!*

> **I have known the joy and pain of deep friendship. I have served and been served. I have made some good enemies for which I am not a bit sorry. I have loved unselfishly and I have fondled hatred with the red-hot tongs of Hell. That's living.**
> *Zora Neale Hurston*

New Plates
Anne

I am going to buy some new plates. Disgracefully bright, flamboyant plates. Plates with loud colors, bold patterns, plates that evoke sunshine, eating in the open air, holidays, foreign designs.

For forty years I have used plates received as wedding presents, functional white plates, earthy brown plates. A few have been broken over the years, but not enough to justify adding to them or changing them for something a little more inspiring.

Until now.

What has made the difference? Well, last week I sold a silver rose bowl, also a wedding present given to me by my boss on that auspicious occasion in 1955. It is beautiful and for years I cleaned it regularly and displayed it on the dining table either empty or filled with fruit, and admired its elegance and symmetry. However, over the last few years my lifestyle has changed so much that it does not fit in among my wooden sculptures and objects, baskets of shells and stones, chestnuts and pine-cones. It has been stuck at the back of a cupboard collecting a deepening layer of dust and tarnish.

So I decided to sell it! I took it to the Silver Vaults in London where a blackened label underneath indicated it had originally been bought. I was thrilled when they offered me what seemed like a fortune. I was told that in 1955 it had probably cost about $18—a very handsome and generous gift.

Now I am adamant. This money is not going to disappear into housekeeping or paying the bills. It is mine to spend as I want, and I intend to use part of it to buy some new flamboyant plates, which will bring a disgraceful pleasure into my future eating.

Come eat with me!

Generation Game
Anne

My son was very proud of me at his wedding in June. I had invited my cowriters in the Hen Co-op to share in the celebrations. "Do we have to be well behaved, or can we be disgraceful?" they asked me. I wasn't quite sure what they had in mind, but I assured them that they should just be themselves, and I crossed my fingers and hoped they wouldn't put disgracefulness to shame forever by being too silly or undignified. I could not let my son down on this auspicious occasion!

There were over a hundred guests, family and friends, in an informal setting and my Hen friends blended in with the others during the moving ceremony and on the lawns in the sunshine before the reception. They were dressed in a variety of colorful and flowing clothes and looked very beautiful, as usual. In one of the official photos my son and his bride are flanked by three of us on either side, and they look as pleased as we were.

These special friends queued up in well-mannered fashion to be greeted by bride and groom, they talked to other friends and cousins, they were not too conspicuous as they moved around together. Even when they were photographed individually it did not create too much of a commotion on the well-tended grass with a backdrop of trees and bushes.

Then the six of us moved to a children's merry-go-round nearby and we clambered noisily on to the tiny model horses and birds, waving and grinning, guffawing and posing, and I thought, "I hope not too many of the guests can see me in my smart party dress shrieking from the back of a child-size horse". Finally we moved to a huge metal sculpture of a gorilla and we put on fierce grinning scowls to match and compete with the statue; a sight most unbecoming in elderly matrons. However, this passed smoothly and without too much comment.

It was during the meal, when dessert was served to the seated guests, that I felt I should have been more strict when setting boundaries for their behavior. My son, visiting the tables as dutiful host, came back to me at the head table and exclaimed with undisguised delight, "Do you know your friends have ordered cream to go with their pudding?" The only table apparently to do anything so outrageous, as this was not part of the set meal!

True, they didn't climb in the trees like the small children, but sometimes it was difficult to differentiate between the behavior of these unstoppable adults and their small counterparts.

My son obviously enjoyed the privilege of six disgraceful authors together at his wedding, especially as one of them was his mother. I was very proud of him and proud to be one of the six.

Johanina

Telling Stories
Mary

What would my life be like now if I'd never done anything disgraceful, if I'd never ever thought about growing old disgracefully?

I would never have left my husband, or got a divorce at the age of 58 after 34 years of marriage. I would be a widow now, feeling disappointed with myself and my life, living on a small pension and probably watching such things as soaps on TV in the middle of a sunny afternoon, trying desperately to get something interesting going on in my life!

I certainly wouldn't be sitting in front of a word processor trying to write a book about old age with five other old women and calling ourselves the Hen Co-op! That's what I am doing now—isn't that disgraceful?

Growing Old Disgracefully was a great title for our first book but sometimes I have found that it can provoke the wrong kind of expectations! When people try to imagine old women growing old disgracefully they are tempted to picture us performing outrageous stunts like hanging midair on the sails of a windmill or enjoying an orgy of shared lovers in a hen coop!

But for us "Growing Old DIS-gracefully" stands for the opposite of "Growing Old GRACEFULLY" —which was what our mothers aspired to. It was the one rule they passed on to their daughters, being, for them, the only lesson that women were allowed or needed to learn about getting older! But now I feel I live in a different world. I am part of a new generation of women—alive to tell my own story as honestly as I can.

And this *is* what is so disgraceful—an old woman telling her own story in her own way, with honesty, with no holds barred, as best she can.

Maybe I have been lucky in many ways. For example there was a lot of hope about in the 1960s and 1970s, when I was looking for my second chance, when I realized that in another three or four years our four daughters would have left home and I would be left on my own in a loveless marriage for as far ahead as I dared to look. There were new ideas and opportunities as well around at that time. So I got my second chance. I got an education and then I got a job that I enjoyed doing. And I got out of the loveless marriage before it was too late.

Most important of all, just at the right time when I needed it, there was the Women's Movement. I learned whatever I could from the younger women there, often feeling, I remember, that the Women's Movement was for *them*, that it had come too late for me.

But certainly it was what I had learned from the Women's Movement that gave me the words and the courage to lead the first Growing Old Disgracefully Courses at the Hen House soon after I retired in 1988.

How could I ever have anticipated what was to follow? It has been a whole renewing of my life—at the age of 65! And now, at 70, I am looking at myself—full frontal—asking myself the question: "So what am I doing that is so disgraceful?"

Well, first of all I'm spending my money! At 70 I think this is what nest eggs are for and I've no intention of letting worries about paying for residential care spoil what time is left for me to enjoy myself. So I'm not saving money and I'm not saving my best clothes either—I'm wearing them! And I'm writing a novel! A novel. It's about six old women who happen to be staying for Christmas at the same cheap hotel by the sea. After dinner in the evening they leave the two husbands with the TV while they take turns to tell each other stories about their lives, honest and disgraceful stories, and their lives are changed as a consequence.

I hope I shall have both the time and the stamina to finish it before I die and you, who are reading this book about growing old disgracefully, I hope you will be clamoring to read it!

Even so I find it hard to put into words what I so passionately feel needs to be said at this point. I am saying that stories need to be told, women's own stories—not as happy-ever-after stories but with honesty, as we have truly lived and felt them—with anger and with love, with pain and with joy, sometimes with disappointment, sometimes with hope.

But why? Why is all this looking back at our lives necessary when it is the present and the future we of the Growing Old Disgracefully philosophy should be most concerned with?

Because in the telling, in the writing and the sharing of our stories there can be so much more than pleasant reminiscence—because, as so much of my own experience has taught me, telling your own story, sharing it with other women, can be a way into self-awareness that can come in no other way. And because, with self-awareness comes the possibility of change, of self-development and of renewal, no matter how old we are, no matter at what age the process begins. And it *is* a process, not an event—a process where there can't really be any endings.

And sometimes now I realize that my own story will not have an ending that can tie everything together, that could provide a satisfactory sense of finished business for this stage of my life. That is unlikely to happen because there are still so many things I haven't done yet, things that I said I would do last time when I wrote my contribution for the last chapter of *Growing Old Disgracefully*. I was going to sort out all my old photographs and treasures and talk to my daughters and twin sister about all the things that are most difficult to talk about—and I haven't done any of them yet!

Perhaps for now it's just as important to be able to laugh when I forget the word or the name I want to say, when I lose something (as I do so often), when I don't hear properly what is being said (and that happens even more often), when I wobble a bit or need some extra time to get up the steps…!

And it would be good if there was someone to share the laugh with, but there often isn't and there won't be. That is when I shall need to hang on hardest to all the lessons I've learned from *Growing Old Disgracefully*.

There is one lesson I hope I shall be able to hang on to till the very end—that when I see something as lovely as the golden leaves of the silver birch outside my window now, I shall still be able to say, "Yes—I know when I am happy."

Warts and All
Shirley

Have you noticed how much energy we use in destructive, negative ways? I certainly do. Let me give you an example.

I have a tiny little balcony to my second floor flat which is crowded with tubs of flowers and herbs. Oh, they've been planted all right, but they seldom grow to their full harvest. More often than not these tender shoots, planted lovingly in anticipation of coming seasons, get eaten by grubs, snails or greenfly. So much for the gardening therapy for old people so highly recommended by all the philosophers and doctors.

Each morning I repeat my little ritual on waking which includes a trip to the balcony to observe the growth of my tender shoots and seedlings. But, instead, the first thing I usually see is the slimy trail of snails. How do they get there? How do they climb so high, I mutter, as I go out in my nightie to pry the pots apart and remove whole colonies of snails from their furtive hiding places.

If you were to look across from your window opposite at the little old lady, who then can be seen throwing the snails to the garden beneath, you might be tempted to call for the straitjacket. I have this surge of sneaky energy as I hurl them as far as I can, giggling all the while. You might object, but I'm not prepared to give up the battle against the creatures who deny me the joy of the potential blossoms and waste the money I've spent on the plants. No, I'm not mad, but I do feel brazen and that's not a bad feeling for an old woman, so give a little cheer instead.

That's cruel, I hear you say. So negative. How can you be proud of doing that? Well, I'm not exactly proud of the vindictive streak that swells up in me in those repeated forays. But what I am happy to own up to is the energy not to give in—that's the other side of the coin. It's the same energy and persistence that I hope to continue bringing positively to everything that matters to me as I grow even older. There is a persistence, too, which is about a determination to survive, to overcome hardship and setbacks that may come my way. No, I'm not going to give in apathetically to injustice because my voice might be sidelined by those who prefer the invisibility of the old. My voice can still join the chorus of others and be counted—and not discounted. I refuse to stop being a thorn in the side of those whose actions I disapprove of. I *will* continue to fight for the things in which I believe until I die.

And another thing I'm happy to own is the ability to laugh at myself in the snail episodes, not caring that others might disapprove or think me cranky. Too long in my youth did I modify my behavior for fear of offending those whose attitudes were inflexible. Nor am I going to take seriously my cousin's remark: "I hope you're happy about all those women who've left their husbands because of your first book!"

If I had stuck with my old patterns of behavior and not begun to grow old disgracefully I'd never have experienced sharing the pleasure of writing the first book with my sister Hens, of writing this second one, of being part of workshops and readings everywhere, or being on the radio and TV, and receiving all those wonderful letters and remarks which are a constant delight and surprise.

If I hadn't started on that positive path I would not have heard what the 25-year-old bookstore clerk said after a reading in California. "For months I've been feeling blocked. But on hearing you read from your book, I know now how to move on. Thanks." Or my 67-year-old namesake Shirley in Jerusalem who wrote to say she was choreographing a dance to a poem in the book as a surprise for her husband's 70th birthday. Or the glow I feel when, at a workshop, I see old women who had lived a long time alone with their thoughts make connections with other like-minded women and become aware that old age need not be so dreary as they had anticipated.

Does all this sound smug? The temptation to be so is easily punctured, as when my grandchildren tell me I can't make macaroni cheese "as nice as Daddy does," and, oh yes, when my friends criticize me for killing snails. OK. So I'm not perfect. I may even be disgraceful sometimes in the dictionary sense of that word, such as when I'm murdering snails. But I'm using the same energy, the same persistence, the same self-mockery and imperfections, in negative and positive directions.

That's what I'm doing that's disgraceful, being an imperfect person, complete with all my foibles, not being decimated with that knowledge, and using my energy to take advantage of whatever opportunities come my way. Sometimes that charge of energy comes out negative, and at other times it is spontaneously positive, such as when my five dear sister Hens and I decided, crazily, on the spur of a moment five years ago, to write a book.

> **The best time in life is always now because it is the only time there is. You can't live regretting what's past, and you can't live anticipating the future. If you spend any amount of time doing either of these things you'll never live at all.**
> *Germaine Greer*

I'm Not Finished Yet
Edith

Of course I'm not finished yet; anybody looking into this room can see me still scribbling away, desperately trying to get this piece, "my last words," finished on schedule. Scribbling is what I do; everything written in longhand first, then painstakingly transcribed onto the typewriter. The first deadline has already been missed. That is what generally happens, but I do eventually turn up at the finishing line with the completed work. You may well ask why, why has this become my signature tune? Do I mind turning up at each session, prefacing the reading of my latest incomplete piece with, "I'm not finished yet"? I used to care very much, even being reluctant to read the little I had written. As the writing process has eased, I take it in my disgraceful stride as do my sister writers who are no longer surprised by my tardiness. They have become so inured to it, that if I ever did arrive with the requisite work on schedule, the shock might be too much and I am not willing to risk it.

But then I'm not finished yet in the main areas of my life either. I'm at a turning point, a recognizable one. I am fully aware that the death of my husband in March 1994 created the major shift in my life, putting me in a different place. After all the years of struggling to establish an independent identity, all the planning put into maintaining a separate space for myself; none of this is needed any longer, none of it is any longer relevant. With his death this identity was thrust upon me; the long struggle is over. This is not the way I would have chosen to accomplish it, but the choice was not mine.

While the inward grieving goes on, the rational part of me has had to come to terms with my changed situation and I need to make decisions about the future. Was being on my own indicating a different path or was I to carry on as before but minus a partner and just to drift? Should I be taking the alternative way, making determined efforts, within the constraints of health and finance, to follow the Growing Old Disgracefully philosophy? The answer is obvious. I've been discovering things about myself in the slow writing process. Stimulated during these last five years by the interaction with my sister writers and affected also by my husband's protracted illness and eventual death, I feel determined to change aspects of my life.

I have to recognize the new focus that these last five years have given to my life via the writing process. My complaints about the struggle to produce results are real; the difficulties in the early stages are even more so, but the challenge as well as the accomplishment have made important contributions to my life. I don't want it all to disappear. While there are no expectations to continue writing in that context, I do want some form of that particular activity to go on and on and on, along with the challenges … the challenges which should keep me physically and mentally on my toes.

Women have always had to improvise in new circumstances. It starts with menstruation and goes on right through life. It's when they haven't needed to face these challenges any longer that they settle down to growing old gracefully and invisibly. Since I have no intention of conforming to that pattern, I expect my disgraceful old age will throw up new challenges for me to deal with from time to time. One of the first of these is on the horizon now; it's the computer. I'm tired of my old typewriter and want this more up-to-date equipment, especially as I have been advised by one of those whiz kids that I'm definitely too old to learn new tricks. I have every intention of proving him wrong. If I am to go on and on writing, the scribbling has to stop, then the new technology can take me onward.

So, if you turn on your modem, linked to the computer, my E-message will come up on your screen: *"I'm not finished yet"*!

CHAPTER EIGHT

Guidelines for G.O.D. Groups

Shirley

If you've read this book so far and agree with its general thinking, you may wish to start growing old disgracefully in the company of like-minded women. This chapter, therefore, is intended to help groups get off the ground and to provide some tips and exercises so that people can get to know each other in a supportive group *and have fun* at the same time.

It takes energy and enthusiasm to start a Growing Old Disgracefully group, but those who take up the pen or telephone to contact others can take pride in the fact that this first courageous act may be the beginning of a whole new adventure. *At your age!* How disgraceful!

You could try writing an introductory letter or phoning the people you know to discuss suggestions as to dates, possible meeting places etc.

When writing, it is best to send recipients a stamped, addressed envelope. The cost of postage, photocopying and phone calls may be prohibitive for some but, where possible, others can reimburse the sender later by some sort of kitty or benefit in kind.

Some groups meet in church halls, local community centers or quiet pubs where it is possible to spend a couple of hours in a side room spinning out just one drink or a light lunch! Others may prefer to take turns to host meetings in their homes. People may have to travel long distances or have transport difficulties, and these are factors to take into account when choosing a meeting place.

The First Meeting

Everyone is probably feeling quite nervous, meeting new people, not knowing what to expect. But, congratulations on having come so far.

The object of this first meeting is, therefore, twofold: to get to know each other, and to make practical arrangements for future meetings.

Getting to Know Each Other

There are many ways of doing this but here is a group exercise you could try which focuses on and starts the process of discovery. No one needs to be the leader but one person does have to volunteer to start and another needs to volunteer to take notes of people's needs and expectations so that they are not forgotten.

Sitting in a circle, each person in turn says:

• her name

• something about the history or reason for having been given that name

• where she lives

• why she's come

• what she would like from the group.

It may seem impossible at first to meet all individual expectations but compromises can be made, priorities negotiated and the group discussions need not prevent individual friendships blossoming simultaneously. This first discussion will help you to make the future program.

Practical Arrangements

As well as getting to know each other, use some of the time at this first meeting to make the following practical arrangements for future meetings.

How often is the group going to meet? This is entirely up to your group. If members want primarily to share ideas and get down to intimate discussions, then the meetings need to be fairly frequent in order to build up trust. If, on the other hand, you are all meeting just for a social chat, you may wish to get together less frequently. Also, if group members are quite scattered, it may be difficult to meet often.

How will group members keep in contact with each other? Do you know the names, addresses and telephone numbers of everyone who attended the first gathering? If some are not already members of the Network, they will not be on your original lists. Remember to check whether members wish their names to be disclosed to others.

Who is going to do the administration stuff? Keeping members and potential members aware of dates and venues is crucial. This job can be done in turn or on an organized rotation basis, shared by a few or arranged through a telephone tree (where each person has to phone one other member). It is important not to overload one person with this task, unless someone is eager to take it on. By sharing jobs there will evolve a sense of belonging and mutual regard, which is what the group is all about. Whatever you do, people should not leave this first meeting without knowing when and where you are meeting next, who is doing what, what costs may be incurred, whether you are going to invite others to join the group.

Hopefully everyone will feel exhilarated by the meeting. But don't give up yet if the meeting wasn't quite what you expected. Each person has an individual responsibility to make it work. If you are shy and unable to assert your needs the first time, perhaps you can do it at the next meeting. Please give it another try.

Points to Consider

During the first or second meeting before you get in too deeply, the group needs to discuss what rules it requires to function well. These are the sort of things that need to be addressed:

Confidentiality: Are your discussions going to be honored as confidential? By this we mean that no one will go out gossiping about what people might reveal in the group. Where people get together in these sorts of groups, they may divulge bits of their lives which, on reflection, they would have preferred keeping to themselves. Without a promise of confidentiality, it will be difficult to establish an atmosphere of trust and respect.

Inability to attend: What will happen if people cannot attend a forthcoming meeting? Should there be a designated person to whom you can send your apologies? Alternatively, you may prefer to contact the hostess or another, to confirm that you *are* coming.

Costs: If anyone incurs costs, for example, for the hire of a room or for postage, then what arrangements will be made so that they are not out of pocket?

Transport: Are carpools necessary to get members to meetings? Who needs them? How will they be arranged?

Refreshments: If you meet in each other's homes, how will you contribute towards the cost of refreshments? Our advice is to keep it simple.

Smoking: Should this be allowed or not allowed? We'll leave this for your group to make its own decision.

Subsequent Meetings

So far, so good. Don't underestimate your shared achievements in getting this far! Congratulations to those who did the arranging and to the others who are still motivated to making the group work.

Here is where the consolidation of the first discussions begins to take place. Perhaps there are some women who didn't come to the previous meeting. Do they need to introduce themselves and you to them? Someone needs to offer to lead the meeting as you continue to discuss the needs and purpose of the group. This can be done by different people at each meeting. (See: Leading a group, page 235.)

Some people are likely to have forgotten some or all of the others' names. So why not have another round of names and interests? You could do it in one of the following ways:

• Say your name, but add a positive adjective such as: 'I'm Jane, Jolly Jane', or 'I'm Valerie, Valuable Valerie', 'Margaret, Magnificent Margaret,' and so on. It doesn't do any harm to be immodest occasionally, particularly if you want to become disgraceful! Keep on saying the names until you all feel confident, then test it out! Introducing yourself this way can produce laughter and helps to break the ice.

• Sitting in a circle, throw a ball, teddy bear or cushion, to another person in the group as you give your name. Keep on until everyone is familiar with all the names.

You will find lots of suggestions for introductory games in books. Of course, you can also invent your own games!

Creating a Program

Before a program of activities is devised it would be useful to find out what skills and interests there are in the group. Why not try a round like this:

Each person in turn says: 'I'm good at ...', or 'I like doing...'

You will be amazed at what people are likely to say. After an initial reserve, groups of women who consider themselves quite ordinary, invariably fill in the gaps in the above sentences with topics like: massage, gardening, computers, knitting, cooking, sewing, writing short stories, watercoloring, grandparenting, swimming, golf, politics, and so on. In this way members' special interests and experiences will become apparent. Those who describe themselves as 'just a housewife,' will hopefully begin to identify and acknowledge the skills involved in these roles and begin to feel more confident about them. As the group continues, there will be opportunities when skills can be shared.

In addition to the topics that have emerged, others will arise and you may also wish to invite new women in to introduce new subjects. But as you begin to trust each other you may feel able to discuss not just the fun subjects but also those that give concern like loneliness, coping on a pension, the problems of vacationing alone, the thrills and risks of being a grandparent or an in-law, widowhood, bereavement and so on.

Not all discussions need to be done in the big group. It's often very good to start a meeting occasionally or frequently by talking in twos or threes. Living alone as many of us do, it is not uncommon to spend days without talking to anyone on more than a superficial level, like at the newsdealer's or post office. So these twos or threes can provide an important starting point, a time in which you can both listen and speak.

Many people (with the best of intentions) often rush in with questions and solutions while the other person is in full flow, which can result in a deflection away from the subject that the talker wants to explore. A useful way to overcome this is to make a rule that each half of the twosome has, say, 5 or 10 minutes to talk without interruption, and then to continue with the discussion. You can follow this with an equal period for the second person. It's amazing how hard it is to avoid interruption, but this way ensures equal time for everyone.

It is fun to share other activities too, such as dancing, singing, painting, childhood games, cooking, writing and so on. You don't have to be brilliant at any of these things but so much fun can be had by letting your hair down and just having a go with others. It is by talking and playing together that we get to know each other and learn what problems, joys and skills we have in common.

Themes

The chapters in this book are written around themes and you may wish to explore them yourselves in your own groups. We find that discussions of such themes add to the depth of self-knowledge, friendship and enjoyment within the group.

So, here are some triggers for developing our themes in your own way in your groups. Feel free to adapt, change and develop your own ideas.

The exercises for each of the seven themes are best done in pairs and can be shared later with the rest of the group, for more observations.

1. Expectations and Reality

The aim of this exercise is to give you a starting point for reflection on how far life has come up to your expectations. Ask yourselves the following questions:

• Can you remember what your expectations were when you left school?
• What did you most want to happen in the next five years?
• Were you ambitious?
• Did you know what you wanted to do?

Think over the answers you've given.

Now think about your life today. Has it measured up to your expectations?

• Not at all   • Yes
• Not much   • Even better than
• Pretty well

2. Choices

One way to think about the important choices you have made in the past is to make a road map of your life, marking the decision points, such as: leaving school, marriage, death of a loved one, work, moving home, divorce and so on. Your map can be depicted by lines, graphs, circles, illustrations or exclamation marks.

Discuss whether with hindsight you would have chosen differently.
Do you think you have choices now?
What might limit those choices? For example:

• money
• health   • transportation
• where you live   • family needs
                      • friends

Are there things you can do to change any of these?

3. Sexual Matters

Write an advertisement for a lonely hearts' column, describing yourself and what you would want in a partner in no more than 50 words. Write a serious, truthful one and then another for fun.

Sharing these advertisements with the others in the group can bring lots of laughs.

4. Conflicting Needs

Where would you put yourself on this line?

Too few
demands
on me

Just right

←——————————|——————————→

Too many
demands
on me

Where would you *like* to be on this line?

If you're not where you would like to be, what can you do about it?

If you decide you want to make changes to get the balance better, start with small steps and make them specific. Work the steps out with a partner in the group and write them down. Reward yourself when you manage to do them.

5. Loneliness

When were the times in your life when you felt most lonely? How did you deal with it at the time?

Are you lonely now? To what degree:

- Never
- Seldom
- Sometimes
- Often
- Always

Is there anything that you can do to change the degree of your loneliness? Make a list of things you might be able to do to change things.

Decide on a first step—then do it!

6. What Lies Ahead?

So, how *can* you make the most of what lies ahead?

There are some things that are hard and can't be changed, but there are others you might be able to do something about.

Mark two columns on a sheet of paper. Write at the top of one 'Things that can't be changed,' and at the top of the other 'Things that could be changed.'

Discuss these lists with a partner and/or in the group and you may well find ideas to lessen some of the problems which seemed intractable.

Then, ask yourself:

• 'In the circumstances in which I live now, what things still give me pleasure?'

• 'Do I know when I'm happy?'

7. Being Disgraceful

Think about one thing you might like to do in the near future but which you have held back from because others might think it disgraceful.

In pairs, ask each other: 'What is stopping you from doing it?'

Then, having answered the question, ask another: 'Do you need any help to overcome those things that are stopping you?'

Having identified what help you need, see if you can ask for it. You may be surprised at the outcome!

Sharing these thoughts may help give you courage to do those disgraceful things (they may not even seem disgraceful to the others), and you may also find that obstacles can be overcome.

Other Activities

All right. You're now part of a group. What else can be done to help the group develop in the months and years ahead?

Writing

We have such a store of memories, of our lives before electronic gadgetry, of friends and acquaintances long dead, of wartime, of memorable experiences. Before senility threatens those memories and before we die, it will be good to reminisce with others from a similar era and trigger even more reflections on our lives. What's more, if we have children and grandchildren they are usually fascinated to hear these stories from before their time—that is if we haven't bored them silly with them already! Anyway, you now have a whole new audience.

Here is an opportunity to write down some of your memories. Most people instinctively say they can't write and think no one would be interested in their story. How wrong they are. We are all unique and if we are growing old disgracefully, we must be survivors for one reason or another. Most women, we find, have a fund of interesting stories to tell, which they tend to undervalue with misplaced modesty.

Begin with, say, half an hour discussing a particular topic. This could be followed with fifteen minutes for everyone to write. Longer writing time may overwhelm some people at first but it can always be extended if members decide they want it. When the writing time has ended, members can each be invited to read their piece out to the group. You will not only learn about each other but come away from the group with heads buzzing with ideas and surprises. We're prepared to guarantee that there will be a lot of laughter along the way and probably some tears also. And this is how support begins to build within the group.

Here are some ideas for topics to write about on different occasions. Of course members will also come up with their own.
- a wartime memory
- what I was like as a child aged 5, 10, 15
- my first paid employment
- mothers and daughters
- my first date
- making ends meet
- my favorite smells
- school days
- love and marriage
- things I hate

- sex and sensuality
- jealousy
- holidays I've enjoyed
- feeling lonely
- anger

If ideas for discussions and shared writing ever dry up, you could plan to read the same book, watch a particular controversial TV program or go to see a film, then discuss them in the group. We can promise you interest, stimulation, laughter, support and friendship as a result.

Painting, Drawing, Collage

We're not suggesting the fine art to which some people may aspire in professional classes. What we find women enjoy in Network groups, is to be involved in art which is not going to be judged. One way of achieving this is an exercise in which everyone paints or draws with their nondominant hand, so that even skilled artists are not at an advantage.

Another fun thing to do is to collect magazine illustrations and paste them up into a collage—which could depict scenes from your real or fantasy life!

And another example which can provide a great deal of fun is to decide on a particular scene, then divide members into three groups, each with a collection of painting materials (the cost of which you have all contributed to). One group will paint the foreground of the scene, another the mid-ground, and the third group paints the distance. When you're all finished display your work and try matching the three sections. Just see what happens!

Games

Laughing together is such a release. Here are some fun games we recommend for promoting laughter. They should keep you going for hours!

- Write limericks.

- Make up stories by each saying one sentence in turn. Or instead of a complete sentence, everyone contributes just one word at a time. You can make it tricky by having to start the next sentence or word with the last letter of the previous sentence or word.

• Have a good old singalong. Decide first on a theme (love, animals, the weather, flowers) and then each person in turn thinks of a song on that particular theme. Everyone joins in singing it, before you move on to the next person.

Dancing

Play some favorite music—jazz, folk, country and western, classical etc., and interpret the music by moving as it takes you. Kick off your shoes, loosen up and let your hair down—but first move the furniture to avoid bruises!

Assertiveness Exercises

Think of an incident in which you wish you had responded more assertively, or imagine a scene, such as with a negligent salesperson, and reenact it differently. For further examples see Edith's story and Mary's questionnaire on pages 115 and 130.

And So On...

There are lots of books which describe group games. But don't ignore the skills and ideas within your own group. Check them out. You'll even have fun just remembering the games of your youth.

Leading a Group

Finding the right way to make a group stimulating yet comfortable enough for even the shyest to come forward with their views is easier said than done. Usually some form of agreed structure for the group makes it safer and sometimes it requires a leader to get the thing going. Some people believe they are born to be leaders and the rest can only follow. We don't agree. While some people do have qualities of leadership, we hope that Growing Old Disgracefully groups will promote people's self-confidence and give everyone the chance to experiment in leading a group at some time.

But we aren't talking about leadership with a capital L. What we mean is that if you are to avoid meetings that always slip into vague, unfocused talk (which can happen and is enjoyable in its own way), someone has to take responsibility for starting off a discussion on a particular subject. If you want your Growing Old Disgracefully group to offer you something more than all those cosy, traditional women's groups which degenerate into coffee and gossip and nothing else, then you need an agreed upon structure and a leader or facilitator. But that doesn't mean that it has to be the same person each time. It is infinitely preferable to take this role in turn.

One way of doing this is for one member to suggest a subject for discussion, say Mothers, then that person starts it off. At the next meeting another deals with another subject and so on. You may like to decide on a topic at one meeting in advance to give people time to think about it.

Having a facilitator is a way of avoiding a vacuum in a meeting where everyone is leaving it to someone else to start. Often the more difficult part of a discussion is to ensure that everyone who wants to, can find a space to say what they need to. Some people may want to stay silent for a while until they feel more confident and some may resent that. On the other hand resentment may occur if the same person is always putting her oar in.

Getting the balance right is the difficult bit and that may need either some leadership qualities in one person, or a cooperative effort in handling these issues in a nonexplosive way.

Troubleshooting

Not all groups go smoothly all the time. Sorting out opposing styles and personalities can be difficult but it would be a shame to let resultant strong feelings distract the group from its positive, disgraceful purpose.

If a few guidelines are agreed for the group discussion time some problems may be avoided.

1. It is preferable for all to listen when one person is talking. It can be very distracting if individuals start making comments to their neighbors.

2. Allow lots of time for talking in twos and threes, especially at the beginning of meeting as this can help people to feel relaxed in the group. Many people find it hard to talk in a large group, especially if they feel overwhelmed by another member.

3. Appreciate all the different life experiences that will emerge. Each person's life and viewpoint is valuable and important to them. We can learn so much by listening to each other.

4. Take turns leading the discussions, thereby discouraging one person from dominating.

5. While members who are living alone or who are unhappy may welcome the opportunity to talk at great length about their difficulties, Growing Old Disgracefully groups are not intended to become therapy groups. There is a danger if members think they can help in all cases where other women are needy. Sympathy and a willing ear are no substitute for appropriate professional help; sometimes it will be better sisterly support for those in need if you encourage them to find specialized help rather than becoming too involved in their burdens.

We can hear you saying. That's not what we've joined the group for. You're right. But, by being aware of some of the risks likely to cause damage, and at least being able to discuss them openly in the group—perhaps before people get hot under the collar—the group will grow all the stronger.

Viable Group Size

If the group does not seem viable because there are too few of you, the group may decide to try to find additional members. Our experience is that it is best done by word of mouth. Advertising in local libraries, for example, requires one person to be responsible for responding, and it may take a long time to explain what is meant by growing old disgracefully—and some people could assume quite the wrong thing!

The number of people attending each meeting may vary because of personal commitments, health, etc. so we would recommend that a core number of members should ideally be no less than six, with twelve being an optimum number. Intimacy will develop best where numbers are not excessive.

Sometimes a group gets cosy together and is resistant when a new member wants to join. If some people's instinct is to close the door to newcomers, consider how any of those present would feel if *she* were denied access to the group. After all, the Network groups are about supporting each other and giving ourselves strength to live life more fully.

When numbers do grow too large for comfort, consider splitting the group. But that can be painful where friendships and a group cohesiveness have developed. Consider the possibility of having some small and some large group events so that everyone can feel included. But the program will have to be accommodated to suit the numbers. For example, the discussion can be in pairs rather than the entire group, or perhaps a guest can be invited or a video shared in order to focus on less intimate matters.

Endings

The way sessions end is really important.

So, it's best to try to find a way to bring activities or discussion to a close, preferably on a high point. Sometimes the ending happens naturally and at other times someone may suggest something that in time could become a happy group ritual.

How about a game, song or dance, such as we've outlined in this chapter? Finding a way to touch each other can be good, especially as so many women are often deprived of touch as we get older and lonelier. This is why dancing is so good. But we hope everyone will be sensitive to individual likes and dislikes as, while some people may welcome a hug, others with a natural reserve may resent what seems to them to be inappropriate familiarity.

We hope that, as everyone gets to know one another, you may all dare to have a group hug, which is the way we, the Hen Co-op, regularly finish our get-togethers.

But there is no one definitive way to end a session. We hope that each group finds what feels comfortable for them.

Growing Old Disgracefully,
the Hen Co-op's first book, can be found at

The Hen Co-op
Flat 3
4 Highbury Place
London N5 1QZ